YOUR
NOVEL
PROPOSAL

FROM CREATION TO CONTRACT

The Complete Guide to Writing
Query Letters, Synopses and
Proposals for Agents and Editors

BLYTHE CAMENSON AND MARSHALL I. COOK

WRITER'S DIGEST BOOKS
CINCINNATI, OHIO

Other fine Writer's Digest Books are available from your local bookstore or direct from the publisher.

Visit our Web site at www.writersdigest.com for information on more resources for writers.

To receive a free weekly E-mail newsletter delivering tips and updates about writing and about Writer's Digest products, send an E-mail with the message "Subscribe Newsletter" to newsletter-request@writersdigest.com or register directly at our Web site at www.writersdigest.com.

03   02   01   00   99   5   4   3   2   1

Library of Congress Cataloging-in-Publication Data

Camenson, Blythe.
   Your novel proposal : from creation to contract / by Blythe Camenson and Marshall J. Cook.—1st ed.
     p.   cm.
  Includes index.
  ISBN 0-89879-875-2 (hardcover : alk. paper)
  1. Fiction—Authorship. 2. Fiction—Authorship—Marketing. 3. Authors and publishers. 4. Book proposal. I. Cook, Marshall. II. Title.
PN3355.C26 1999
808.3—dc21   99-23558
                                                  CIP

Editors: David Borcherding and Michelle Howry
Designer: Sandy Kent
Cover designer: Stephanie Redman
Production coordinator: Kristen D. Heller

Acknowledgments

Blythe Camenson and Marshall J. Cook would like to thank the following authors, agents and editors for their insightful comments and advice on the world of writing and getting published.

And for those who provided letters and synopses—professionals and students alike—a special note of thanks.

AUTHORS

Carla Anderson (Jessica Barkley), James Scott Bell, Marilyn Campbell, Robyn Carr, Tom Clancy, Julie Goldman Connard, Anne Kinsman Fisher, Dick Francis, John Grisham, Peggy Hoffman, Michelle J. Hoppe, David Kaufelt, Stephen King, Dean Koontz, Barbara Parker, Paxton Riddle, James A. Ritchie, Kiel Stuart, John Tigges, Robert W. Walker, Karen Whiddon

AGENTS

Kathleen Anderson, Scovil, Chichak, Galen Literary Agency, Inc.; Julie Castiglia, Julie Castiglia Literary Agency; Jane Chelius, Jane Chelius Literary Agency; Rob Cohen, The Cohen Agency; Russell Galen, Scovil, Chichak, Galen Literary Agency, Inc.; Anne Hawkins, John Hawkins & Associates, Inc.; Richard Henshaw, Richard Henshaw Group; Frances Kuffel, Jean V. Naggar Literary Agency; Nancy Love, Nancy Love Literary Agency; Evan Marshall, The Evan Marshall Agency; Martha Millard, Martha Millard Literary Agency; George Nicholson, Sterling Lord Literistic, Inc.; Lori Perkins; Perkins, Rubie & Associates; Pesha Rubinstein; Pesha Rubinstein Literary Agency, Inc.; Peter Rubie; Perkins, Rubie & Associates; Cherry Weiner; Cherry Weiner Literary Agency; Nancy Yost; Barbara Lowenstein Associates, Inc.; Susan Zeckendorf; Susan Zeckendorf Associates, Inc.

EDITORS

Nancy Bereano, Firebrand Books; Marjorie Braman, HarperPaperbacks; Jennifer Brehl, Avon Books; Kent Brown, Boyds Mills Press; Ginjer Buchanan, The Berkley Publishing Group; Kent Carroll, Carroll & Graf Publishers, Inc.; Paula Eykelhof, Harlequin Toronto; Laura Anne Gilman, Dutton; Wendy McCurdy, Bantam Books; Michael Seidman, Walker & Co.; Karen Taylor Richman, Silhouette; Anne Savarese, St. Martin's Press; John Scognamiglio, Zebra Books; Elisa Wares, Ballantine Books

PART TWO . . .95

THE PACKAGE

CHAPTER SIX

SUCCESSFUL SYNOPSES, *123*

CHAPTER SEVEN

CRAFTING THE COVER LETTER, *187*

▼

INTRODUCTION

First a word to those of you who have written a novel. Congratulations!

Stop and savor your achievement. Lots of people think they can write a novel, but most never do it. It takes hard work and a belief in your story, even in the face of the world's indifference. You must write your novel without any assurance of reward, other that the deep satisfaction and the joy of doing it.

"The profession of book writing makes horse racing seem like a solid, stable business," John Steinbeck said. When he started out, Steinbeck didn't know he'd end up famous. He couldn't have foreseen that his work would be read and treasured by millions. What sustained him through the times of agonizing doubts? He wanted and needed to tell his story.

"Writing a novel is a terrible experience," Flannery O'Connor once said, "during which the hair often falls out and the teeth decay." She was only half kidding.

Red Smith, one of America's finest sports writers, has the most-often-quoted line about the difficulty of the task: "There's nothing to writing. All you do is sit at a typewriter and open a vein."

Why do we do it?

"I write books to find out about things," Rebecca West said.

"You're not hunting your Big Story," Robert Moss insisted. "Your Big Story is hunting you."

Dean Koontz describes that need this way: "I was writing from the age of eight, but I didn't know that I needed to do it until I was about twenty. By the time I was twenty-five, the act of writing itself was nearly as necessary to me as food."

We do it for the sake of the story, yes, and also because writing is the most amazing sort of joy, what Richard Wright called "heightened living." We write because writing lets us live fully, openly, meaningfully—if not always peacefully or happily. We write because we have a hard time imagining not writing.

"Writing is the only thing that . . . when I'm doing it, I don't feel that I should be doing something else instead," Gloria Steinem said.

We don't wait to be inspired to write. We write to be inspired.

GETTING IT PUBLISHED

Ah, but you don't just want to *write* your story. You want people to *read* it, the more people the better. And you wouldn't mind if they paid you for the privilege.

You want to get your novel published.

You must now make a second commitment. Getting your novel published will take the same sort of creative problem solving, the same determination and persistence, the same refusal to quit that you brought to writing the book. Just as you learned and are learning how to write with skill and power, you now must learn how to market your work effectively. You need to know how to write good query and cover letters, how to create an effective, selling synopsis, how to package your proposal and get it into the hands and to the attention of the right people.

This book will show you how, step by step, with guidance from agents, editors and novelists.

But you'll need to follow your own lights as well. "Write about things that are important to you, what you believe in, what you have passion about," advises Kent Carroll, executive editor of Carroll & Graf publishers. Others will echo his advice in the pages of this book.

"The main thing is to keep writing," notes Wendy McCurdy, an editor at Bantam Books. "Keep writing and remember that it takes time."

In the chapters that follow, we'll show you your publishing options and help you select wisely. You'll learn how to give your novel the strong marketing effort it needs and deserves.

You'll be ready to become a published novelist.

Are you ready to start the journey? Are you willing to do the work? Then read on.

PART
ONE

THE APPROACH

CHAPTER
ONE

YOUR PUBLISHING OPTIONS

"**Writing is not the lottery. New writers have to be realistic about what it takes to get published. But there is one similarity to the lottery: You have to play to win.**"   —Lori Perkins, literary agent

C lose to sixty thousand books will be published in the U.S. this year. That's more than 160 books a day! We'll spend about twenty billion dollars buying those books. Book publishing is big business.

Although popular fiction will account for more than half of all books sold, only about 10 to 15 percent of those sixty thousand published titles will be fiction. A few fiction titles will account for a disproportionate number of sales: fifteen to twenty novels will each sell a million copies or more. In a typical year a handful of writers will account for two out of every three novels sold. You know the names of these titans. Before you read on, see if you can name the seven writers who have dominated fiction sales in recent years.

Ready? They are, in no particular order,

John Grisham
Stephen King
Michael Crichton
Tom Clancy
Danielle Steel

Mary Higgins Clark
Dean Koontz

No surprises there. Before you change your name to King, Clancy or
Crichton, though, keep in mind that the market uncovers new and
talented writers each year. Recent examples include Carolyn Chute (who
had to borrow money for postage to submit her first manuscript to a
publisher), E. Annie Proulx, Larry Baker and Amy Tan. Talented writers
are still breaking the publishing barrier, and these folks prove it.

WHAT'S SELLING
Children's books dominate the top categories of best-selling books.
1. children's age 9-12 trade paperback
2. children's age 4-8 trade paperback
3. children's age 4-8 hardcover

Romance novels are the fourth-largest category; romances account
for more than half of all mass-market paperbacks published each year
(around eighteen hundred titles).

Note: Trade paperbacks are the larger, more expensive variety.
Mass-market paperbacks are the smaller and less expensive books.

After three nonfiction categories fill the nos. 5, 6 and 10 slots,
fiction takes four of the remaining top positions.
7. general fiction, trade paperback
8. general fiction, hardcover
9. general fiction, mass-market paperback
10. mystery, mass-market paperback

WHO'S PUBLISHING ALL THESE BOOKS?
Seven media conglomerates, along with perhaps a dozen of the largest
independent publishers, produce between 75 and 85 percent of all
books published in North America today.

After the "Big Seven," another twenty-two hundred publishers do
enough business each year to qualify for listing by the U.S. Depart-

ment of Commerce. *Literary Market Place*, the industry reference published by R.R. Bowker, lists another eighteen thousand to twenty thousand smaller and independent publishers.

Regardless of size, we can categorize book publishers as:

- national/international
- regional and small press
- university
- organizational/sponsored
- subsidy
- cooperative
- book packagers/producers
- self-publishers
- electronic publishers

Which route should you take to publish your book? Let's look at your options and the circumstances under which you should consider them.

THE NINE PATHS TO PUBLICATION
1) National/International Publishers

The seven megacorporations that dominate book publishing in North America are (with some of their major publishing imprints in parentheses):

1. Hearst Corporation (Avon, William Morrow)
2. News Corporation/Rupert Murdock (HarperCollins)
3. Pearson PLC (Penguin, G.P. Putnam, Berkley)
4. Viacom (Simon & Schuster, Pocket Books)
5. Bertelsmann AG (Bantam, Doubleday, Dell, Dial, Random House, Knopf, Modern Library, Ballantine)
6. Time Warner/Ted Turner (Little, Brown; Book of the Month)
7. Holtzbrinck (Farrar Straus & Giroux; St. Martin's Press; Henry Holt)

ADVANTAGES

The big boys can get wide distribution and a spot on the shelves at Borders, Barnes and Noble, B. Dalton Bookseller, Waldenbooks and the large independents. If you seek a wide, national audience and perhaps even a slot on the best-seller list, you'll need to crack one of these giants.

Commensurate with their size and the expected sale of your book, the big corporate publishers pay relatively large advances. (That's an advance against royalties, a prepayment before you actually begin to earn royalties from sales of your book. We'll discuss this in more detail in chapter nine, where we enjoy the good news of publication.)

DISADVANTAGES

Because they're visible and powerful, the national and international publishers get mountains of submissions. They can afford to be extremely selective about the projects they look at—let alone publish. Competition is fierce. Only commercially viable proposals, presented professionally, stand a chance. That makes it tough, but it doesn't make it impossible.

Often, the larger the house, the less control you'll have over the editing and publishing of your book. **Approach:** Find a literary agent. We'll tell you how in chapter two.

2) Regional/Small Presses

America is blessed with thousands of wonderful book publishers, most of whom never see the light of the *New York Times Book Review*— much less the best-seller list.

ADVANTAGES

Small presses can afford to take chances because they can survive on considerably smaller sales than their more cumbersome and better-known colleagues.

They are often superb at servicing speciality and special interest markets and specific regions of the country. If your novel deals with a

---

Desperately Seeking Silhouette

S ilhouette Books is one of the major publishers in North America, producing several lines of romance novels—including Silhouette Special Edition and Silhouette Desire. And yet, Silhouette is but one small book in a huge corporate library. Silhouette and Harlequin, another big publisher of romance novels, are part of one of six divisions of Allyn & Bacon Publishing Company. Allyn & Bacon is, in turn, a subsidiary of Simon & Schuster. Thanks in part to another subsidiary—Pocket Books—Simon & Schuster is the largest publisher in the U.S., with about two billion dollars a year in sales. Simon & Schuster is so big, they have a senior vice president in charge of strategic planning, and they use words such as *synergy* to describe their internal corporate linkages.

Simon & Schuster was absorbed by Paramount (formerly Gulf and Western), which, in turn, was bought out by Viacom in 1994. (Publishing accounts for just 21 percent of Viacom's net revenue, the rest coming from films and television, cable TV, theme parks and broadcasting.) Viacom then merged with Blockbuster Inc. And that, friends, is the face of book publishing, corporate style.

Ultimately, editors at Silhouette Books answer to stockholders of Blockbuster. So, when book publishers act like megacorporations, fixated on bottom-line profits, it's because they *are* megacorporations, fixated on bottom-line profits. ▲

---

red-haired, left-handed Virgo trying to find love in the mountains of northern Idaho, you might just find a small press specializing in books featuring red-haired, left-handed Virgos in northern Idaho.

Many small presses are founded and run by writer-editors who are disgusted with the offerings on the best-seller lists and are dedicated to publishing outstanding fiction. Find one of these to love your book and you'll have a passionate champion.

Unlike the big commercial publishers, regional and small presses are open to unagented submissions.

DISADVANTAGES

There's no such thing as a typical small press, but you would expect to find that a small press publishes fewer titles (as few as one per year), has a smaller pressrun for a first edition (two thousand to five thousand copies) and features small or nonexistent advances.

Many small presses lack the firepower to get national distribution and the kind of push needed to generate big sales. However, lots of small presses are looking for a breakout book to take them national. Yours could be the one.

APPROACH

Most small presses prefer to be contacted by the author rather than an agent. Find the name (and correct spelling) of the appropriate editor (who is often also the publisher) and send your proposal directly.

CAUTION

Don't think for a minute that the small press is a place to try to peddle second-rate material. They may be smaller, but they are no less (and in many cases are more) discriminating than the big guys.

3) University Presses

University presses generally serve a well-educated and discriminating audience. Most university presses specialize in particular subjects, but many also publish mainstream books.

ADVANTAGES

The university press has better access to certain specialized and niche markets. Most enjoy fine reputations. Your project will get professional care.

A Few Good Small Presses—and How to Find More

You may have never heard of some of these and other independent publishers, but you may be a lot more familiar with some of them by the time your journey to publication is over. Here are a few good small presses:

- **Black Heron Press**

  Jerry Gold, P.O. Box 95676, Seattle, WA 98145

  Publishers of *The Inquisitor*, *The War Against Gravity* and other experimental novels. Established in 1984, Black Heron averages four titles a year with a pressrun of one thousand.

- **Black Sparrow Press**

  24 Tenth St., Santa Rosa, CA 95401

  Established in 1966, they publish a dozen titles a year. Average pressruns are twenty-five hundred copies for a first printing.

- **Cross + Roads Books**

  Norbert Blei, P.O. Box 33, Ellison Bay, WI 54210

  A new press that has started strong with *The James Dean Jacket Story*, *I Thought You Were the Picture* and other titles.

- **Ecco Press**

  Daniel Halpern, 100 W. Broad St., Hopewell, NJ 08525-1919

  One of the biggest and best independents, Ecco Press, established in 1971, publishes twenty-five titles a year—poetry, fiction, criticism and nonfiction. Average pressrun is four thousand.

- **Keokee Press**

  Chris Bessler, P.O. Box 722, Sandpoint, ID 83864

  Book publication was an outgrowth of their fine regional magazine, *Sandpoint*. The breakout book for Keokee was *Pavlov's Trout*.

- **Papier-Mâché Press**

  Shirley Coe, 135 Aviation Way #14, Watsonville, CA 95076

  Established in 1984, Papier Mâché emphasizes women's issues. They publish seven to nine titles a year, with pressruns of six thousand to twelve thousand.

- **Pushcart Press**
  Bill Henderson, P.O. Box 380, Wainscott, NY 11975
    You don't know small press unless you know Henderson and Pushcart (established 1973). They publish the annual *The Pushcart Prize: Best of the Small Presses*—a wonderful anthology—and sponsor an annual editors' book award for manuscripts overlooked by commercial publishers. Eight titles per year, with a variable pressrun.
- **Savage Press**
  Mike Savage, P.O. Box 115, Superior, WI 54480
    Savage Press published Marshall's recent novel, *The Year of the Buffalo*, in 1997. Savage also publishes a literary magazine, *The Northern Reader*.
- **The Spirit That Moves Us Press**
  Morty Sklar, P.O. Box 720820, Jackson Heights, Queens, NY 11372-0820
    Established in 1992, Spirit publishes one title a year, with a pressrun of six thousand. Their most recent was an anthology, *Patchwork of Dreams: Voices From the Heart of the New America*.
- **Steerforth Press**
  105-106 Chelsea Street, P.O. Box 70, South Royalton, VT 05068
    Established in 1993, up-and-comer Steerforth publishes eight to ten titles a year, with an average pressrun of five thousand.

And the man who keeps track of it all . . .
- **Len Fulton**
  Dustbooks, P.O. Box 100, Paradise, CA 95967
    Len Fulton is godfather and midwife to the small press movement in America. He self-published his novel, *Dark Other Adam Dreaming*, and applied what he learned to helping other publishers. He produces a monthly magazine reviewing small press publishers, and for thirty-three years he has published *The International Directory of Little Magazines & Small Presses*, the source for independent publishers. If you want to know the independent press, you've got to get to know Dustbooks. ▲

DISADVANTAGES

Most university presses publish little or no fiction—though there are exceptions to every rule. Few university press books break through to a large, national audience. Advances range from nonexistent to small.

APPROACH

As with the small and regional presses, most university presses will accept proposals directly from the author, and many shy away from agents—who don't have much knowledge of or interest in university presses anyway.

4) Organizational/Sponsored Presses

Many organizations have their own publishing arms, and some will sponsor or subsidize projects of special merit and interest to their constituents. For example, the Adoption Awareness Press, a division of the Musser Foundation, Cape Coral, Florida, published *Chasing Rainbows: A Search for Family Ties*, about a woman who finds her birth mother at about the time the daughter she had given up for adoption finds her.

ADVANTAGES

You've got a novel that would really appeal to folks who build their own airplanes for fun? Try the EAA (Experimental Aircraft Association) in Oshkosh, Wisconsin. They can reach those folks better than anybody.

Every once in a while, a novel issued by an organizational or speciality press breaks through and finds a national market. Can you name Tom Clancy's first publisher, for *The Hunt for Red October*? It's Naval Institute Press, which nearly sank trying to keep up with the demand.

DISADVANTAGES

You think your book might have a chance with somebody other than those hobby plane builders? You'll probably be better off with a larger press.

APPROACH

Find the appropriate name on the organization chart and make an initial inquiry by letter or phone before launching a proposal.

5) Subsidy Publishers

You've seen the ads that announce "Publisher Seeks Manuscripts"? Next time you see one, turn the page.

Subsidy publishers (also known as "vanity presses") prey on writers frustrated by their failure to find a publisher and on folks who just don't know any better. They act like commercial publishers, "evaluating" your project and offering a publishing contract. But when it comes time for money to change hands, it's your money—a lot of your money—going to the publisher, instead of the other way around.

ADVANTAGES

You do get a book published. Some subsidy houses offer minimal help with marketing.

DISADVANTAGES

You pay and pay and pay. Editing is often minimal to inept. Production is often shoddy. Libraries won't buy your book. Reviewers won't touch it. Often all advertising and publicity are left to you. And you don't even own the books!

APPROACH

Never.

6) Cooperative Publishers

Some publishers ask the author to participate in the costs of producing the book. That means you put up part of the cost of printing and binding and thus share the risk with the publisher. (In subsidy publishing, you pay the entire expense, plus a hefty markup for the publisher's overhead and profit.) Or you may be asked to supply camera-ready copy, meaning you're responsible for editing and typesetting your manuscript or having that work done.

Many small publishers work in all three categories, publishing some books on a commercial basis, some with a co-op deal and still others on full author subsidy.

ADVANTAGES

A lot of these guys do a fine job for a reasonable charge. Many can help you with publicity and distribution. Their imprint on your book and a place in their catalog will help, not hurt.

DISADVANTAGES

You're still, essentially, paying someone else to publish your book, and the stigma of vanity publishing attaches itself to some cooperative publishers—especially the ones who also issue books on a subsidy basis.

APPROACH

Use caution. Get some help in evaluating any contract you're offered.

7) Book Packagers/Producers

This relatively new breed of publishing is growing rapidly. A book packager or producer acts as an intermediary, selling a concept to a publisher and then contracting with the author to create the book. Often the author works for a set fee rather than receiving royalties.

Most book packagers deal with nonfiction projects, generally as part of an established series of books. For example, Marshall has published two books through CWL Publishing Enterprises—a book on motivating workers for the Macmillan/Spectrum "10 Minute Guide" series and another on time management for the Adams Media Corporation business book series.

ADVANTAGES

The author is assured of publication and a prearranged payday. The author gets a byline and national/international exposure.

DISADVANTAGES

No chance to cash in if the book sells big, and the packager generally retains the copyright. Also, the opportunities for fiction are scarce.

APPROACH

Once you've had a few things published in magazines, a book packager may seek you out to do a nonfiction book. Aggressive and smart packagers attend writers meetings, read the acknowledgments from books in fields that interest them, and call universities and colleges to find out who the experts are in various fields.

If a packager hears of your work and makes you an offer, consider it. But the likelihood of a packager (or anyone else) approaching you to write a novel is next to zero.

If you have a good nonfiction idea, especially one that would fit into a publisher's existing series of books, you could send a proposal to a book packager, just as you would to the publisher.

8) Self-Publishing

Edgar Rice Burroughs did it. So did Zane Grey, Mark Twain, Stephen Crane, Virginia Woolf, Edgar Allan Poe and James Joyce. They and thousands of other writers have taken their work directly to a printer and come home with boxes full of books. But these days, it's very risky, and it can carry the same sort of stigma that attaches itself to subsidy and cooperative publishing.

One of our favorite self-publishing success stories is The Dunery Press, founded by Charles and Natalie McKelvy. They're successful freelance writers who became disgruntled with the world of commercial fiction and started publishing and marketing their own fiction, one novel from each per year. They've found a small but loyal market for titles such as *Holy Orders* and *Clarke Street* (by Charles) and *The Golden Book of Child Abuse and Other Works* and *Party Chicks & Other Works* (by Natalie).

ADVANTAGES

You're in total control of the project, from idea to finished book. Every buck that comes in goes into your pocket. You own the books. You might just sell a lot of books. Occasionally a self-published novel breaks out in a big way. *The Celestine Prophecy* and *The Christmas Box* provide two recent examples.

Nonfiction books stand a much better chance of self-publishing success, however, especially when the author has extensive knowledge of the subject (or access to the people who do) and a direct line to potential book buyers. Tom Klein thrilled packed houses with his illustrated lectures on the loons of northern Wisconsin. When he self-published *Loon Magic*, he had himself a best-seller—and the beginning of a career in publishing.

Successful or not, you'll also learn a lot about publishing in the process.

DISADVANTAGES

You have total responsibility for the project, from idea to finished book. The books sit in your basement, garage or family room until or unless you do something to get them sold.

Every dollar that goes out comes from your pocket, and almost all of the money flows out before any starts coming in. You have to be willing to invest a lot of money—and possibly lose it.

Most of the self-published books that do find a wide audience are nonfiction. Examples include *The Joy of Sex* and *What Color Is Your Parachute?* It's much, much tougher to market a novel on your own. You'll have to learn a lot about publishing in the process.

APPROACH

With extreme caution. Prepare a proposal and evaluate potential markets, just as you would if approaching an agent or editor. If you've been turned down by commercial publishers, figure out why before you take the risk.

9) Electronic Publishing

There's a lot of publishing activity on-line these days. Some writers are offering their wares on-line—everything from poetry and journal entries to sample chapters or complete manuscripts of novels. Some try to sell their material, while most simply give it away to anyone who hits (or wanders into) their sites.

"Cyberpublishing" is emerging as an alternative delivery system for novels—if not a completely new medium. Folks are buying and downloading material, including novels, and either reading them on-screen or printing out their own copies of the work. The option exists, but nobody seems to be making any money publishing books this way.

Will such "cyberbooks" ever become more than a fad? It all hinges on feel. Folks love the snappy links and instant searches, but few so far like to read book-length material from a computer screen. It's just not as comfortable or convenient as taking that old tattered paperback to bed or to the beach or on the subway.

Should you seek cyberpublication? We urge caution. Some fly-by-night on-line publishers promise payment for your words, fail to deliver, and then vanish into cyberspace. Many new electronic publishing companies offer to post your book for free and pay you royalties. When you get to the fine print, though, you learn that there are many hidden charges—such as uploading fees—and no guarantee that anyone will ever pay to download your book or that you'll ever see a royalty if they do.

Additionally, while the copyright laws apply to material published on-line—just as they do to any other kind of publication—they are at this time much harder, if not downright impossible, to enforce. Once your material is out in cyberspace, you may have lost all control over it.

▲▼

For the remainder of this book, we're going to assume that you want to get a commercial publishing contract for your novel. You believe in your book, and you want someone to pay you to publish it. Read on to learn how.

CHAPTER
TWO

THE SEARCH BEGINS:
FINDING AGENTS AND EDITORS

"Publication of early work is what a writer needs most of all in life."

—Erskine Caldwell

T he majority of agents and major publishers are nestled within a
few square miles of downtown New York City, but a trip to
Manhattan is not a requirement; in fact, that wouldn't be a good idea
at all. Agents and editors are very busy people with full schedules.
Stopping to greet every new writer who decided to drop in would
mean that no work would get done. Query letters wouldn't get answered; manuscripts wouldn't get requested and sent out; acceptances
(and rejections) wouldn't get passed on.

"Every day we have people who call or drop by and want to meet
with us on the spur of the moment," agent Frances Kuffel explains.
"They don't realize how busy and scheduled our lives are. These
people are often abrupt, demanding and condescending. Don't they
realize that the people concerned are going to weigh that in [when
deciding] whether they're going to take a person on as a client [and]
whether they're going to stick with someone when things get bad? It
would be hilarious if it weren't such a trial."

A face-to-face meeting isn't a necessary step in the process, although
at the appropriate time and place—at writers conferences, for example—it can be the best way to find an agent or editor. More on that
later.

ORGANIZE YOUR SEARCH

Finding an agent and getting published is not a speedy process. It could take a year, often more, to land a contract. Marketing your work can feel like a full-time job—and it is. Writing the novel is only half the picture.

In the course of a year, you could contact dozens of agents and editors, sending out an equal number of query letters, synopses and full and partial manuscripts. How embarrassing—and counterproductive—it would be to receive a rejection from Agent X in January and again in June, the latter including a note with a barely civil, "Didn't I turn this down before?"

Let's face it. Very few writers send out two or three query letters and land an agent or a book contract on their first mailing. With so many submissions circulating, it's important to keep accurate track of them.

Start by setting up a directory in your word processor for submissions on each project. Make a file with a form or chart listing all the agents and/or publishers you plan to contact. As you send your material out, note what you have sent next to each name—e.g., query letter, chapters one through three, synopsis—and the date you sent it. It is also a good idea to note where you found the particular agent or editor—at a conference or on page 28 in a market guide, for example.

As material comes back—the rejection letters (and yes, those will come—it's part of the process) and requests for more material—note the response and when you received it.

With a tracking system set up, you are now ready to start your approach.

FOUR WAYS TO APPROACH PUBLISHERS
1) "Over the Transom"

Publishers still refer to an unsolicited manuscript as an over-the-transom submission, even though years ago builders stopped putting above the doors those little windows which supplied ventilation. (Did writers back then really throw their manuscripts over the transom, and then run?)

Big houses get one hundred or more over-the-transom manuscripts every week. The editors didn't ask for them. They don't have time for them. They might not even have desk or shelf space for them. And they certainly don't want to wade through a thick manuscript to determine its market potential.

So they don't.

They might simply stuff it into the self-addressed stamped envelope (SASE) with a form rejection and wing it back unread. If there's no SASE, such a submission will probably just hit the recycle bin.

More likely, the editor will never see an unsolicited novel at all. It will probably land on the "slush pile" of an overworked, underpaid editorial assistant, who must screen out all but the rare project that might be worth the boss's attention.

No one knows how many unsolicited manuscripts publishers receive. A few years back, *The New York Times* estimated the odds against publication of such a project at fifteen thousand to one— which would mean that two or three unsolicited manuscripts would actually make it to publication in a given year.

We hear about the occasional success story, of course. *Jonathan Livingston Seagull* began life on a slush pile, for example. But we hear about these stories because they're so rare, not because they're the norm. We don't recommend making over-the-transom submissions.

2) Direct Referral

Sure, a nice introductory letter from your pal Stephen King wouldn't hurt your chances one bit. An endorsement from the author you met at a writers conference or took a workshop from might also help get your project onto the editor's desk, especially if the editor knows and respects that writer's work. Folks go to those conferences and workshops to learn their craft and to become savvy marketers. They also go to meet the right people. You'll learn more about the benefits of conferences in upcoming chapters. We'll even teach you how to make known you have a referral.

But solid endorsements are hard to come by. And they aren't the only way to get your novel published.

3) Proposal

Instead of sending a manuscript, market-savvy writers send a proposal. In later chapters we'll describe for you the elements of a successful proposal—query letters, synopses and/or chapter outlines, and sample chapters—and teach you how to create winning pitches.

The purpose of the proposal is to get the editor to ask for the rest of the manuscript. That way, when that manuscript arrives, it bypasses the deadly slush pile and goes directly to the editor for evaluation.

4) Agents

For working with the big New York publishers, having an agent is the best way to go. Read on and learn how to go about finding one and evaluating if he's the right one for you.

WHAT TO LOOK FOR IN AGENTS AND PUBLISHERS

To begin with, pinpoint agents or publishers who handle, specialize in or publish the kind of book you've written. It sounds like an obvious guideline, but many new writers overlook it. The shotgun approach doesn't work here. Mistargeting your submissions is a waste of everyone's time and your postage. Sending fiction to a publisher who puts out only nonfiction or submitting your romance novel to an agent who handles anything but romance won't bring you any closer to your publication goals.

Agent George Nicholson of Sterling Lord Literistic says, "I'm bothered by writers who don't do their homework and writers who don't really know what an agent can and cannot do for them. I have to do a lot of homework to know where to submit manuscripts for the writer. Knowing the reputation of the agent or agency [and] what they require in the way of submissions is part of the homework a writer must do before even submitting to an agent. Too often the writer doesn't research who to submit to and very often sends material to the wrong people."

THE IDEAL EDITOR

John Cheever once said, "My definition of a good editor is a man I think charming who sends me large checks; praises my work, my physical beauty and my sexual prowess; and who has a stranglehold on the publisher and the bank."

So much for wish lists. But there is one item on Cheever's list that merits serious consideration. Your editor (as well as your agent) should definitely believe in your book. While lavish praise might not always be forthcoming, tepid levels of enthusiasm won't generate you many book sales—or future contracts.

Your editor should also be someone with whom you can work. It's rare that a first-time novelist is handed a book contract and shortly thereafter, the book goes off to the printer. An editorial stage almost always comes in between. Editors make notes, and writers are expected to make revisions. An editor's insight into your work, ability to make constructive suggestions, and understanding of what sells and what doesn't coupled with your flexibility, talent and belief in your editor's good judgment will make a winning team.

For that first novel, you might not feel you have a lot of room for argument or dissatisfaction. Let's just get that baby to print. But if once you have established yourself you find you're butting heads with your editor on important issues, it might be time to take your work elsewhere.

THE IDEAL AGENT

Best-selling author John Grisham says, "Having an agent is the difference between being published and not being published." Insert the word *good* in front of the word *agent* because, actually, having no agent is better than having a bad agent.

What makes a good agent? In addition to handling the type of work you write and believing in your work, your agent must share your vision, understand your career goals and be willing to support them.

Most agents (and editors) are not looking for one-book wonders. They want clients who are steady, serious writers who will produce a number of books over time.

It's important that you meet the agent's requirements, but it's equally important that the agent meets yours.

Ideally, your agent should be a member of the Association of Authors' Representatives (AAR). The AAR publishes a canon of ethics, and members are expected to adhere to them. One of their tenets is that AAR members are prohibited from charging reading fees. AAR members also don't charge excessive amounts for photocopying, faxes and other administrative expenses. Legitimate agents make their money selling your work, not from fees they collect from hopeful writers.

If an agent isn't an AAR member, it doesn't mean he or she is unethical. Often new agents just starting out haven't applied yet for membership or haven't put in enough time or made enough sales to meet AAR's requirements. And probably some are not joiners, just as some writers don't join writers associations.

To receive a list of member agents, the AAR code of ethics, and a brochure describing the role of an agent, send a check for $7 (made out to AAR) to:

> AAR
> 10 Astor Place, 3rd Floor
> New York, NY 10003
> phone: (212) 353-3709
> www.bookwire.com/aar/

Be sure to include an SASE—a no. 10 envelope with fifty-five cents postage (to cover up to two ounces). The AAR will not be able to provide you with information regarding the types of manuscripts different agents consider, nor will they be able to tell you which agents handle specific authors. This information is discussed later in this chapter.

Here's a checklist of what to consider when making your choice of agent.

_____ The agent is an AAR member.

_____ The agent charges a standard 15 percent commission for domestic sales and does not have any hidden charges and fees.

_____ The agent has a sufficient track record, having sold books to established publishers.

_____ The agent's contract protects both parties' interests and has terms for a satisfactory dissolution of the relationship, if that should become necessary.

_____ The agent will send your manuscript out to more than one publisher at a time.

_____ The agent is familiar and skilled with the auction process.

_____ The agent agrees to stay in touch with you on a regular basis and doesn't object to your calling.

_____ The agent will send you copies of all rejection letters.

_____ The agent will involve you in all phases of negotiations with a publisher and will not accept or reject any offers without consulting you.

_____ The agent's client list is not so huge that you will get lost in the crowd.

_____ The agent is equipped to handle subsidiary rights, such as movie options, book club deals, foreign rights and electronic rights.

WHAT AGENTS DO FOR YOU

Agents serve as the initial screen, filtering out inappropriate, inept and near-miss projects. Good agents match projects with prospective publishers, saving the editors from having to wade through worthy submissions that just aren't right for their imprints.

Agents even know which editor at a given house is most likely to give you a receptive reading. When Marshall's second agent, Marian Young, represented one of his novels, she decided to send it to Charles Scribner's Sons first. Why? The protagonist was a convert to Catholi-

How to Recognize a Podunk Agent

Having what Bantam Books editor Wendy McCurdy calls an "absolutely, lousy, podunk agent" can really hurt a writer. McCurdy says, "A podunk agent is somebody from the hinterlands who hardly handles anybody but is just doing this as a hobby. Some just hang out a shingle; there's no licensing, and anyone can call himself an agent and suddenly start deluging editors with faded photocopies and bad manuscripts. [Publishers] get a bunch of junk from them, and it's a shame if you're a good writer, because I'm going to have a lot of [negative] assumptions about that manuscript right away."

And if you're a beginning writer, you might find you can't trust the agent's opinion of your work. Usually, having an agent take you on validates you, tells you you're good enough to approach publishers. But what if you're not really at that point? A new writer might not have enough experience to judge his or her own work. It can be crushing to find out that your "agent" has ulterior motives.

"You're better off on your own than to have an agent who is not reputable," McCurdy says. "Warning signs are that no one's ever heard of him or her, or he doesn't have a list of published authors." (Don't be afraid to ask for that list.)

Something else you can do if you're in doubt is call the editors the agent gives you on that list. McCurdy says she's had a few calls from writers on that subject. "One agent had put my name on his list, and a writer called to see if I had, indeed, bought anything from him. He also asked me if I thought it was OK that the agent was charging him five hundred dollars. I had the opportunity to say, 'No, it's not OK.' I might have bought something from him in the past, but I don't now. However, I haven't had a call from a writer about that particular agent for awhile. I must have been taken off the reference list.

"There are some reputable agents who charge reading fees, but, in general, people don't approve of that. You have to be suspicious, especially if it's exorbitant. No one should ever have to pay five or six hundred dollars to go through this process. I know there are agents who make all their money simply on charging large fees; they never publish anybody, they just make their money off of gullible people. They go through the motions, but they're not really agents."

Writers are not the only people who are hurt by shady agents. Editors find them a real nuisance, taking up their time with substandard or unprofessional manuscripts. "There's no rhyme or reason for what they're sending me," McCurdy says. "There are certain agents that if I get a submission from them, it goes right in the trash can. I don't even respond.

"There's a lot of word of mouth, and that's a good way to find a good agent. You should have heard about him and have no doubt as to his credibility. You should find other authors who have been represented by him or thanked him in the acknowledgments of their books, that sort of thing." ▲

cism—and so was Charles Scribner Jr. She figured he might give it a more sympathetic reading.

That's the sort of thing that good agents know.

"Look at the list of things an agent does," advises agent Lori Perkins, "and tell me you have the time, ability or inclination to handle it all and won't make mistakes that may set back your career in ways you can't even imagine. Or let me put it to you another way: Only a fool has himself for a client."

Your agent will do a lot more for you than simply seek publication. Among the services a good agent performs, Perkins lists:

- sending your work to the right editors
- helping you choose the right publisher and editor
- negotiating the terms of your contract
- representing film, foreign and subsidiary rights
- making sure the publisher keeps you informed on the book's progress

- helping prepare your next project for submission
- keeping on top of financial and legal aspects of your book after publication

Sure, but Perkins is an agent. Isn't her advice self-serving? Not at all. Good agents have no problem attracting good submissions. And book editors will tell you the same thing agents do.

"Find an agent first," says publishing director Marjorie Braman. "It takes much longer to have a manuscript looked at without an agent, because we're inundated."

Agented submissions are often taken more seriously, because an agent's job is to screen out inappropriate material. Agents, in essence, do the first round of selections for editors.

Not all large commercial publishers have closed the doors to proposals directly from authors. "An agent isn't necessary to approach St. Martin's Press," editor Anne Savarese told us, "but you should send your manuscript to a specific editor. Your manuscript will get more consideration that way." Zebra Books is another house open to agentless submissions. "But do your homework," says editor John Scognamiglio. "Know what we are looking for . . . what kinds of books we publish."

Do you want to spend your time doing that kind of homework? Lori Perkins doesn't think you should. "Writers write," she says. "If you're spending the amount of time necessary to keep up with the publishing business, then you are either working for *Publishers Weekly* or you are not as serious about writing as you should be."

Good point. OK, you're convinced. You need an agent if you want a shot at the big publishers. But can you get one?

THE TRUTH ABOUT AGENTS

"You have to have an agent to get published," the saying goes, "but you have to be published to get an agent." Most of us confront this conundrum when we try to publish our novels. Unfortunately, too many believe it and stop trying.

You—yes, undiscovered, unpublished, unknown you—really do

have a chance. Editors have quotas for titles to develop and new writers to discover. They essentially get paid to say yes.

How about agents? Frances Kuffel, of the Jean V. Naggar Literary Agency, told us they're open to new clients. So did George Nicholson at Sterling Lord Literistic, and Jane Chelius, who heads her own agency.

What will induce an agent to take you on as a client? Jane Chelius looks for "wonderful writers whose work I feel personally very enthusiastic about."

Have you already started your search for an agent—without any luck? Here are three possible reasons why:

1. You are mistargeting, sending your proposal to the wrong agent.
2. The agent has a full load and isn't able to take on any more clients just now. (Having said that, if a query so compelling that it knocked the agent's socks off came in, rest assured the agent would make room for that writer.)

And that leads us to point number three.

3. Your query isn't compelling enough. It's poorly written and/or the material it proposes seems flat and unoriginal.

By the time you've finished reading this book, you'll know how to overcome these obstacles. Write with all the skill and passion you can muster. Then you will find someone to love your book as much as you do. It can be done. Nobody was issued an agent at birth, and every novelist was first an unpublished novelist.

HOW TO SPOT THE SCAMS

If after mailing out your query letters you receive a reply saying, "Your book project sounds like it might very well work for us. Send your manuscript along with a $25 (or $50 or $75 or $100 or $150) reading fee," what should you do?

Ignore the letter.

If, after submitting your manuscript, you receive a reply saying,

"Your work shows great potential. I'd love to represent you, but send $100 (or $200 or $300) to whip it into shape," what should you do?

Ignore the letter.

How about the letter that says, "Your book shows great potential but needs a professional's touch. I suggest you contact and work with the following book doctor, then send it back to us." The same day you get a fax from the book doctor, assuring you that his $2000 to $4000 (or higher) fee can be easily charged to your credit card. What do you do? (You're probably catching on now.)

Yes, you should ignore that letter, too.

Most agents and editors are honest, decent people—just as most writers are. But unfortunately, you'll find unscrupulous people in every profession. An unethical agent or editor can leave you no closer to publication—but a lot lighter in the wallet.

The Reading Fee Scam

Some agents charge enormous reading fees—hundreds and, in some cases, even thousands of dollars—before they'll even open the envelope with your manuscript in it. Many of these agents make all or a substantial portion of their income from these fees.

We should note that many legitimate agents now charge modest reading or handling fees. This reflects the volume of submissions they're receiving. However, there are so many agents who don't charge any reading fees—and as members of AAR are forbidden to do so—we suggest you avoid paying even a small fee.

Legitimate agents—the ones who make their money by taking a reasonable percentage of the money they earn for you by getting you publishing contracts (15 percent is the going rate these days)—do their job with no reading fees or other hidden charges.

Hidden Costs Scams

What are some of those hidden charges? Photocopying, postage, faxes, messenger services, phone calls and other related expenses. Basically, these agents expect you to pay for their cost of doing business.

Reasonable photocopying charges can be expected. However, some agents will allow you to copy your manuscripts yourself and forward the copies to them. Other agents, usually those working for large agencies, cover that cost for you or deduct a small amount from any advance they might receive on your behalf. And if they never make a sale for you? "We simply eat the charges," agent Kathleen Anderson of Scovil, Chichak, Galen Literary Agency says.

Here are two examples to illustrate the point.

A student of Blythe's America Online (AOL) course "How to Approach Editors and Agents" unwisely queried and subsequently signed on with a non-AAR agent who was working somewhere in the Midwest. He came for help when after six weeks he was given a bill for $900. The promised bidding war for his novel never materialized; in fact, it's unclear if this agent ever did anything on the writer's behalf. Blythe interceded and was hit with a verbal attack that would make even a political operative blush—but the bill was eventually torn up, and the writer and "agent" went their separate ways. Blythe and her student decided not to take too seriously the agent's threats to blacklist this new writer in New York.

In contrast, Blythe worked with Nancy Yost of Barbara Lowenstein Associates, an AAR agency in New York, for more than four years. During that time a huge number of photocopies of manuscripts and proposals for several book projects were made and mailed out. An equally huge number of phone calls and faxes, some overseas, were also logged in. Blythe didn't receive a bill until a movie option had been sold on her behalf, and then the amount of $116 was deducted from her earnings. Not bad for four years.

Hard-Sell Book-Doctoring Scams

Some agents earn—or try to earn—even higher fees by demanding a professional critique or evaluation of your manuscript.

First, let us qualify this. Not every agent who recommends editing is a crook. Far from it. An agent could be interested in your project but doesn't think it meets publication standards yet. "Get help," she'll tell you. "Come back when you're ready." That is perfectly legit.

But in some cases, certain "agents" are actually earning a commission from the book doctor for every manuscript they refer. In less polite circles, such commissions are called kickbacks, and they're considered sleazy if not downright illegal. In fact, the attorneys general of several states are investigating these operations for fraud. And the attorney general in New York recently shut down one such operation.

Soft-Sell Book-Doctoring Scams

One subtle version of the book-doctoring scam can come after an "agent" has enthusiastically accepted your work and tells you he has sent it out. Several months can go by, and then you receive a call or letter saying that the agent has been unsuccessful at marketing your work. The feedback he has received suggests that your project is still viable, but only if you get a "professional's touch." These agents will never produce copies of those rejection letters and probably will claim that the communications regarding your manuscript were all conducted by phone.

The agent might claim to be very busy, but because he really still likes your novel, he'll do the fixing up for a favor—and for $2000 or more. An inexperienced writer, hooked into the notion that a sale is still possible, might fall for this scam. Don't be that writer.

These scams are really a rotten deal. Those who fall for them and spend big dollars to have their manuscript edited get it back with no guarantee that the agent will look at it, much less agree to represent it.

Again, a referral to a specific editor isn't necessarily proof of bad intentions. But it might be.

Know, too, that some small publishing houses are participating in the same wretched book-doctoring scams. Be wary.

Publishing Contract Scams

Usually getting a contract in the mail from a publisher is cause for celebration. But not always. Sometimes a subsidy publisher will masquerade as a legitimate commercial house, making no mention of payment (yours to them) until you get to the clause buried deep in the contract. Several of these "houses" have been under investigation for fraud and other sundry charges.

The "I-Hear-You're-Looking-for-an-Agent" Scam

A member of Fiction Writer's Connection, the membership association of which Blythe is director, received the following letter:

> I heard you were looking for a literary agent. I specialize in new and unpublished authors, and I would be interested in taking a look at your novel. Please send only the first three chapters and a brief synopsis. The material will be considered immediately, and you will hear from us within three weeks of its receipt. Please include an SASE. If we see promise in your work, we will ask to see the rest of the manuscript. Our agency commission is a standard 10 percent. A list of my personal credentials is included. I look forward to hearing from you.

The reply to the writer's sample said that it showed "considerable promise" and asked her to enclose a check for $95 with her manuscript. "The $95 will be reimbursed after the sale of the manuscript to a publisher."

This agent frequently advertises his services in magazines and might possibly rent lists of subscribers for his mailings. Rule of thumb: Successful, non-fee-charging agents do not have to solicit clients. They don't do mailings, nor do they advertise. Some agents solicit manuscripts simply so they can charge reading fees or refer writers to book doctors and "earn" their "commissions."

TELLING GOOD FROM BAD

So, how can you tell the good ones from the bad? By their fruits shall ye know them. Good agents get contracts for their clients—and make their income that way.

When you encounter writers who have or had agents, ask them about their experiences. Many publications for writers issue warnings. Stay vigilant, and if you have a bad experience, report it to as many groups and publications as you can.

When in doubt, you can ask us. We'd be glad to hear from you via E-mail. Our E-mail addresses are listed in the appendix.

Use common sense to ferret out the bad guys from the good. If you target only AAR agents, you won't have to worry about this. And if you keep in mind that agents earn money by selling your manuscript to publishers and publishers earn money by selling your book in the open market—and neither of them charges the writer for this service—you won't go wrong.

WHAT AGENTS AND EDITORS WON'T DO FOR YOU

Many new writers operate under the faulty assumption that an editor's or agent's main role is to help whip manuscripts into shape so they are ready for the marketplace. These writers figure they got their story down on paper and the rest is up to the publishing professionals. This couldn't be further from the truth, and it's an attitude that prevents many newcomers from ever seeing their work in print.

"I like to see something creative, fresh, well paced, good characters . . . something that is fun to read and thought provoking," agent Martha Millard says. "But I can't tell people how to write. If I could, I'd do it myself. I couldn't write a book for a million dollars. I can help structure a writer's career, but not [her] writing ability. I occasionally will tell a nonfiction author what direction his or her writing needs to take, but I rarely do that with fiction authors."

Agent Pesha Rubinstein agrees that she can't critique the manuscripts that come across her desk. "It's impossible with the volume I'm working with. I don't charge a reading fee, mainly because I don't want to spend my time critiquing when I'm really just looking for clients. If you want to learn how to write, you have to keep on doing it. Go to writers groups, which can be wonderful; attend conferences and seminars. There are going to be a lot of false starts; you just have to keep writing."

WRITERS CONFERENCES

Creating a salable product is only half the process; knowing how and where to market your work is the other half. Set aside a chunk of time to devote to your research. This is not something you can rush through.

There are several avenues to pursue in your search for an editor or agent. Successful writers know how to take advantage of them.

Finding Writers Conferences

Once you become involved in the world of writing, you hear about writers conferences—local conferences, regional conferences, state conferences, national conferences. They are listed in magazines and newsletters such as *Writer's Digest* (the May issue each year gives a state-by-state listing of conferences for the coming year), *Fiction Writer's Guideline* (the newsletter of Fiction Writer's Connection) and *Creativity Connection* (see the appendix for more information); posted on public library bulletin boards; announced on-line and in the newspapers.

There are conferences for mystery writers, for romance writers, for sci-fi writers, for children's writers. There are some that many writers have heard of: Bouchercon; Worldcon; the Maui Writer's Conference; Moonlight & Magnolias; the Southwest Writers Workshop in New Mexico; the Santa Barbara Writer's Conference. Others are known only locally or within their state.

But with so many conferences, how do you judge if it's a good one to attend? By the speaker list, services offered and topics covered.

Speakers

There should be some names on the list with which you are familiar. Good conferences attract good speakers. You should see a selection of New York agents and editors and a selection of published writers. You might not recognize all the names, but you'll be familiar with the publishing houses or writers the agents represent.

You don't need an expensive, three-day affair to find good speakers, either. Even a one-day seminar known only locally can be well worth the time and money if the organizers have invited professional speakers or workshop facilitators.

Most important to consider: If your primary reason for attending is a chance to meet agents and editors face-to-face, then make sure the bios (usually listed in the registration material) reveal interests and specialties that mesh with your own.

Services

Again, the most important service you are probably interested in is the opportunity to meet with editors and agents. Make sure the conference has arrangements for these face-to-face meetings. During these editor/agent appointments, you will get a chance to pitch your project. We cover in detail how to pitch to an agent or editor in chapter four.

Most conferences will set up appointments for you in advance or allow you to sign up on the spot. At a good conference you should not have to worry about grabbing an editor or agent in the hall or sidling up to him or her at the bar—not that it isn't a good idea. Agent Cherry Weiner says, "Hang around the bar where they congregate. Listen to the conversation, and if you have something to add, join in. Then, after a while, ask if you could grab a few minutes of their time to talk to them about your project. Or get someone at the conference who knows them to introduce you. A lot of my clients found me this way."

But, if the conference leaves meeting with an agent or editor entirely to chance, then it's probably a good idea to pass on that conference and look for another.

Some conferences give you the opportunity to have an author critique a partial manuscript of yours. Fees for this service are usually reasonable.

Contests are offered in conjunction with some conferences. Usually, the guidelines are sent to you in advance and the deadline is well before the conference, then the winners are announced at the conference. Winning or placing in a contest at a conference means your name will come to the attention of the "right" people who are attending the conference. It is not uncommon for a contest winner to be approached by an interested editor or agent.

Topics

To get the most out of a conference, especially if you are a new writer, you want to make sure that the conference covers topics that suit your needs and interests. If you write mysteries, maybe going to a conference for romance writers isn't such a good idea.

Or is it?

What if the only conference coming up soon in your area that suits your budget is an annual state Romance Writers of America event and you are most definitely not a romance writer? In fact, it would never even occur to you to attend. We suggest you think again!

The agents and editors who attend these conferences do not necessarily handle only romance. Chances are, especially with the agents, that romance is only one area of interest to them. Again, check out the bios. You might find the perfect romance agent there who also is enthusiastic about mysteries, mainstream and sci-fi.

In addition, though you might find the majority of workshop topics geared toward the romance genre, you will most certainly find topics that can apply to any writer in any genre. Conferences usually cover general topics such as choosing your viewpoint characters, plotting, dialogue, description and a host of others.

Cost

Cost is also a consideration when choosing a conference. For a three-day conference fees range from $200 to $400, but some may be a lot more. This does not include the cost of transportation. The conference fee usually doesn't include the cost of accommodations either. But most do offer a meal package as part of the fee. There are often additional expenses: Some conferences offer you a chance to have a partial manuscript critiqued for an additional amount—around $30 or so, depending upon the amount of material they allow you to submit. Recently, we have heard about conferences that charge for ten-minute appointments with editors or agents. That's unusual; most are free. Some have special events that cost extra (e.g., a special banquet or breakfast meeting).

It can be expensive attending conferences, and writers have to make these decisions based on their budget. The return, however, in the long run, can be well worth it.

Conference Procedures

Most conferences are held in hotels, and it's usually a good idea to come in early so you can check into your room and drop off your bags first. Then, you can find the conference registration booth, sign in and pick up your "welcome package." This usually includes a printed schedule of events, directions and other relevant conference material. This is also a good time to make sure your appointment or appointments with agents or editors have been confirmed.

Networking

The preliminaries out of the way, it is now time to put on your best smile and start networking and making new friends. This, by the way, is one of the best benefits of attending conferences. Most writers work alone. At a conference you get a few days away from your computer—a chance to meet other writers and find out what they're doing. It's a chance to gossip about agents, get referrals and arrange for introductions.

The whole experience can be very stimulating. In a one-day seminar Blythe had organized, she was in the hall when an attendee came running out. The young woman shouted her apologies, then took off toward the exit. Blythe chased after her to ask what was wrong. Out of breath, the woman managed to tell her that the speaker was so motivating, she wanted to hurry back to her novel in progress. Blythe managed to calm her down and talk her into staying for the rest of the day. She wanted to make sure the eager woman would get her money's worth. The woman felt she most certainly had.

Editor Michael Seidman says, "The key is networking, whether it is through classes or attending conferences or whatever works for you. If you meet an agent or an editor, you've got a leg up."

After the Conference Is Over

You're back home and exhausted. Rest a little, but don't procrastinate following up. You might have thank-you letters to write, sample chapters to get out, lunch dates to arrange, seminar material to read, tapes to listen to. Try to get to it right away, while your enthusiasm is still high.

Finally, don't start planning your next conference trip too soon. If you find you are spending more time at conferences than at your computer, something is wrong. At one seminar Blythe organized, a speaker, successful mystery writer David Kaufelt, got up to the podium, looked out over the crowd, and said, "What are you all doing here? You should be home writing!" And he had a point.

GUIDEBOOKS

No one—agent, editor or writer—can attend every conference. Published directories are the next best way to locate potential agents and editors.

LITERARY MARKET PLACE (or LMP, as it is called) is a big, thick annual—the bible for anyone interested in the publishing industry, but usually too expensive for most new writers' budgets. And it's an unnecessary purchase. Available in the reference section of any public library, it contains, among other things, the most comprehensive listing of publishers and agents, but the summaries provided for each are sketchy.

GUIDE TO LITERARY AGENTS, an annual published by Writer's Digest Books, is affordable, distinguishes between fee-charging and non-fee-charging agents, and notes AAR affiliation next to the names of member agents. In addition to listing the subject areas the various agents handle, it also provides information on how they want to be approached.

WRITER'S MARKET, another annual by Writer's Digest Books, lists two thousand magazine markets and eleven hundred book publishers. In addition to editors' names, addresses and phone numbers, *Writer's Market* also lists their E-mail addresses and Web sites. This guide is available as a book or on CD-ROM.

WRITER'S GUIDE TO BOOK EDITORS, PUBLISHERS, AND LITERARY AGENTS, by Jeff Herman, gives brief histories on editors and book publishers and also indicates for each house which editors handle which genres. He lists about eighty agents.

THE INTERNATIONAL DIRECTORY OF LITTLE MAGAZINES & SMALL PRESSES, published by Dustbooks, is *the* resource for finding smaller publishers. It offers a complete listing of the smaller and alternative magazines as well.

NOVEL & SHORT STORY WRITER'S MARKET, another Writer's Digest Books annual, is devoted solely to fiction markets—book publishers and magazines—and also contains articles on writing techniques and getting published.

Genre Market Books

Writer's Digest Books publishes several other genre-specific guides, including the *Children's Writer's & Illustrator's Market* and *Poet's Market.*

In addition to offering places to send your work, these books also function as how-to guides. For ordering information, see the appendix.

TRADE JOURNALS AND NEWSLETTERS

Writer's Digest magazine, *The Writer, the Literary Journal, Creativity Connection, Fiction Writer's Guideline, ByLine, Editors & Writers* and scores of other periodicals directed at writers all provide help in locating agents and editors. Whether through direct interviews or quotes in articles, these publishing professionals share advice and tips and will give you plenty of ideas. It's all yours for the price of a subscription.

Publishers Weekly, another industry bible, is more expensive, but it is available in the reference section of any library. In addition, many of the writers and editors involved with the above-mentioned publications read *Publishers Weekly* and quote from it frequently. They pay for the subscriptions and pass the information on to you.

In *Publishers Weekly* you'll find publishing trends, interviews, new books, hot deals, the *Publishers Weekly* best-sellers list and tons of helpful marketing and writing information. For those with the budget for it, this weekly is well worth its cover price.

Gila Queen's Guide to Markets is a very fine marketing newsletter for writers, with an emphasis on fiction. Theme issues deal with romance, sci-fi/horror and other genres.

OTHER WRITERS' BOOKS

How often have you settled in with a favorite author's new book, opened the cover and scanned the dedication and acknowledgment pages? There they are again. Those heartfelt thanks to a dedicated agent and a talented editor. Wouldn't it be wonderful if you could have that same team working on your behalf?

There's no reason you can't. Chances are the book you're reading is similar in genre to yours. Writers read what they like to write and vice versa. Put down the book, open up your word processor file, and add those people's names to your list of agents and editors to contact.

When you design your query letter—which you'll learn how to do in the next chapter—give this particular version a special opening paragraph. Express your love for that famous writer's work and explain how yours is written in a similar vein. If the book you're marketing is a polished product and your query is captivating, approaching people you have found on an acknowledgments page is even better than hunting blindly through a directory.

What if your favorite author keeps his thanks private? You can still find out who his agent is. Just call the publisher and ask. There are two departments likely to give you that information—the public relations (PR) department and the contracts department. Both must keep record of each author's representative.

ON-LINE

For those of you equipped with a computer, modem and access to the Internet, the Web has recently become a great source of publishing information. Most major houses have Web sites and on-line catalogs. Many writers associations have databases of participating editors and agents open to new writers. Even literary agencies have started producing their own Web sites.

As we said in chapter one, use caution where some of the electronic publication deals are concerned. Probably some of the not-so-legit agents are also taking advantage of the Web for more exposure. Remember that most busy, successful agents don't need to solicit new clients so broadly and don't have much time to spend on-line.

Where do you begin your on-line search? Just fire up your favorite search engine and use any of the following keywords: *writers associations*, *literary agents*, *writers newsletters*, *writers groups* and the name of the particular publishing house in which you are interested. Also, try *Writer's Digest*'s informative Web site (www.writersdigest.com).

In addition, some on-line services, such as America Online, offer active writers clubs and on-line classes in writing and getting published. In Blythe's on-line course "How to Approach Editors and Agents," she frequently invites agents as guest speakers. Through these classes, many of her students have landed an agent. It's a great, inexpensive way to attend a writers conference without ever having to leave home. See the appendix for more information on Web sites for writers and on-line courses.

Selling your book involves much more than just writing it. Attending conferences, networking, reading and surfing the Web are all ways to find the right agents and editors to approach. Once you've identified the ones for you, it's time to turn your attention to *how* to approach them. The next chapter, on query letters, is just the place to start.

CHAPTER
THREE

THE ALL-IMPORTANT QUERY LETTER

"The only thing worse than going into a publisher's slush pile is going into an agent's slush pile." —Kathleen Anderson, literary agent

When meeting new people, a bad first impression can often be turned around as we get to know the person better. But in approaching an editor or agent, you get only one chance to make that good impression—and a strong query letter will help you do that.

The query letter is your calling card, the first step in your approach to editors and agents, and the impression your letter makes will determine how much farther you can go with that person. Simply put, the query letter is a very important piece of writing.

WHAT AGENTS AND EDITORS LOOK FOR IN A QUERY

Elisa Wares, senior editor at Ballantine Books, says, "A well-written query letter is really the unsolicited writer's best foot in the door. You want to sell yourself as well as the idea of your book. A long, involved description of the work to follow is not necessary. The letter should be entertaining, intriguing and informative. You want the editor to read on, not stop with the initial letter. I must admit that if an author bores me in the letter, I will not read his or her submission. It sounds unfair, but writers have no idea how many queries and manuscripts editors get every day. An author has just a few minutes to catch somebody's attention."

Agent Evan Marshall would like to see a query letter describing the project and giving whatever background is appropriate. "I'm most likely to ask to see the manuscript if the letter is professional, moderate in tone and not full of the hype I get in a lot of query letters. Most are amateurish, and I never ask to see the books by those people. Some of the things they do to try to impress me are so silly. 'SEX! OK, now that I've got your attention, here's the hottest book.' It just won't work."

Editor Michael Seidman says, "In query letters I look for calm professionalism. I want to know what the book is, who you are—if that's pertinent—the length and that's about it. Hype is beside the point; telling me my business is beside the point. So is a record of all the friends who loved your work. The best way to get my attention is to write better than anyone else, to know and understand not only my guidelines, but my editorial philosophies—as expressed in the titles we release."

"The two important things in a query are concept and the ability to write," says agent Anne Hawkins. "The funniest query I have ever seen started, 'I'm not so good at expressing myself in words, but....' "

DEFINITION OF A QUERY LETTER

A query letter is a mini-proposal that aims to

- hook the attention of the editor or agent
- describe your project
- tell the editor or agent who you are
- get the editor or agent to ask for more

The most effective query is a straightforward, polished one-page letter. It describes your novel's plot and main characters, focusing on the elements that are most intriguing or compelling; it lists your relevant credentials and publishing credits, if any; and, if you've hit the mark, it will merit you a letter or phone call asking to see the manuscript.

JUST A QUERY LETTER?

"But how can I get interest in my novel based on a one-page letter?" you might be wondering. Wouldn't it be best to send a synopsis, too, and sample chapters? Some of the agents and editors in the market guidebooks say they want to see the whole thing. Why bother with the query letter at all? Let's just send in the manuscript.

In spite of what a market listing might say, sending a one-page query letter really is the most effective—and most economical—approach. It will get you an initial indication of interest—or lack thereof—and will save you unnecessary photocopying and postage expenses.

"Query first," says agent Russell Galen. "Usually, if we're interested at that point, we'll want to see the completed manuscript. I don't ever want to see a full outline or sample chapter unless I've asked for them."

OK, you're convinced now that the query letter is the way to go. But you're probably still resisting the idea of only one page. Why not give them as much information as you can, right up front?

Again, remember you have only a few seconds to grab an editor's or agent's attention. Making him plow through a long letter filled with details won't win you any points. The only excuse to write a query letter longer than one page is if you have scores of credits to mention. But then, these can be sent on a separate sheet that lists your publications and bio.

WHO GETS THE QUERY LETTER?

Send query letters to agents to ask for representation or to editors when seeking publication. Whether you go it alone or seek the services of an agent, it's important to accurately target the right publishing houses, editors and agents for your material. Nancy Bereano, editor at Firebrand Books, says, "Before sending your work out to a particular press, do your homework. Visit bookstores and see other books that press has published; see whether or not your book seems to fit in with what that publishing house has done. Would it be at home there?

Ask for a catalog. Most publishers, Firebrand included, give people catalogs for free. Look through the catalog and see whether you think your book belongs with the others there. It's not magic; it's being informed. Knowing as much as you can in advance of submitting helps make a writer feel much more powerful."

WHEN TO SEND THE QUERY LETTER

Rule of thumb: Write the novel first! Yes, it is tempting to want to get those query letters out quickly. Some of you might be thinking, "Why bother writing the novel if a query letter can let me know so easily if there's interest in my topic or not?" While this is the usual procedure with selling nonfiction books, which can often be sold on the basis of a proposal alone, it won't work with novels—especially novels written by unpublished novelists. We all have to pay our dues and write the book. What guarantee is there that you'll actually be able to deliver what you promise in your query? That's the way agents and editors view it. They all know how much skill and hard work it takes to write a novel. A first-time writer has a lot to learn, and often that first attempt is just part of the learning process.

"Once a query has snagged my interest," says agent Russell Galen, "I ask for, and expect to receive, a completed manuscript. If the writer hasn't previously published a book, such a writer should never query until the manuscript has been completed."

Exception to the Rule

For every rule there is an exception, and publishing is no different. There are some occasions when an agent or editor might ask to see a novel before it's completed. But these occasions generally apply to writers with a track record or a prior relationship with the editor or agent.

Russell Galen says, "More established writers, with at least one book published by a major house, need supply only a portion and outline, or perhaps only an outline. They are actually welcome to approach us in whatever manner is most comfortable, usually a phone call."

If you're already working with an agent, perhaps for a nonfiction project, he or she might be willing to look at a partial manuscript for a novel to offer you guidance and see if you're on the right track.

It could happen for a new novelist, too, usually because of a face-to-face meeting at a writers conference. Although we caution you not to pitch your project until it is finished (see chapter four), once there, it is hard to resist taking advantage of the opportunity for feedback. Some agents and editors will tell you to send your book in when it's done, others will agree to see partial manuscripts. Agent Nancy Yost says she never asks for anything that's not complete "unless it's so fabulous I can't resist."

QUERY-LETTER FORMATTING

A query should look like a business letter. Invest in letterhead stationery or design your own letterhead, but keep in mind it should look clean and simple.

Although desktop publishing software packages provide decorative borders and clip art, allow you to scan in photographs and intricate line drawings, give you multiple typefaces and options to vary size and even shape of letters, these are features that you, as a writer, shouldn't use.

Instead, invest in a nice letterhead stationery that has your name, address, phone number (very important) and your E-mail address, if applicable. The last two will make it easier for an agent or editor to get in touch with you. Nothing is more frustrating than to read a good query and really want to see that manuscript and not be able to reach the writer quickly. It's your job to make it easy for them.

The Greeting

In your first correspondence to an editor or agent, do not address him or her by his first name. Wait for a return letter to see how you have been addressed. If you get back a "Dear Joe" or "Dear Jane" letter, you can follow suit. If the reply is more formal, stick to a simple *Mr.* or *Ms.* . . . *Dear Sirs* and *Gentlemen* have been out of vogue for about twenty years now. If you insist on clinging to tradition, you will annoy the large female workforce in the publishing industry. (See more on letter greetings in chapter seven.)

When addressing your query letter, make sure you include the name (spelled correctly), title (of the person you're addressing—not your book) and address of the editor or agent you're writing. You *must* address your letter to a specific agent or editor.

Editor Wendy McCurdy says, "There are from eight to ten editors at Bantam who handle fiction, from literary or westerns to action/adventure to suspense. Although I would forward submissions to the proper editor if they arrived on my desk, that could add another three months to your waiting time. You should call the publisher's switchboard and ask for an editorial assistant, who can help find the name of the appropriate editor for you."

Also call the publisher's switchboard if you are using market guides as a source for editors' and agents' names and addresses. Market guides, by their very nature, can already be outdated by the time they see print. People change jobs and titles frequently in publishing. Make sure the person you are querying is still in residence.

While you're on the phone, also verify that the agent or editor you are 100 percent sure is a male really is. We'd be willing to bet that agent Rob Cohen gets very annoyed with the "Dear Mr. Cohen" letters she probably receives every day.

Keep in mind that while creating generic form query letters might save you some time with a multiple mailing, a letter addressed "Dear Agent" or "Dear Editor" is no different than those "Dear Occupant" letters you receive in your mailbox every day. And we all know what happens to those.

Here's another reason to avoid generic letters without a name and address on them. Busy agents and editors often scribble their response right on your letter and stuff that into your SASE. How frustrating to get a "Sure, send it in" and have no idea who is requesting it! Equally important, you also want to know who is turning you down. Unless they're kind enough to sign the note in legible handwriting, you'll be left in the dark.

Paragraph Style

You have two choices when it comes to paragraph style. You can indent each paragraph about five or six spaces and leave no lines between paragraphs (this method allows you a little more room when you have one or two lines you just can't bear to cut to fit the one-page length limit), or you can use block style, with each paragraph flush left and one line between each paragraph. When you use block style, the date, address, salutation and closing should all be flush left, too.

You'll see samples of both later in this chapter.

Closings

Close your letter with a *Sincerely*, leave a space to sign your name, then make sure you type your name as well.

Finally, don't forget to run your spelling checker before you print the letter—then set it aside for at least one day before mailing it. You want the chance to go back and proofread for things the spelling checker won't catch—the *their/there*s and *here/hear*s, to name just a few.

SASEs

Always remember to include your no. 10 self-addressed stamped envelope with your query letter for the editor's or agent's response. If you send just a self-addressed stamped postcard (SASP), the editor or agent will not be able to enclose any guidelines they might provide as a matter of course. If you send an envelope smaller than a no. 10 business size, they'll have to cram their full-size response into it. And if you forget the SASE altogether, you might not get a response at all.

Before you fold the SASE into thirds, turn back the flap, so the glued side isn't touching the other surface. Heat conditions in some areas will glue the envelope shut before it reaches its destination, and this can be very annoying for the person on the receiving end.

Agent Susan Zeckendorf stresses the importance of the SASE. "[Writers] should always, always enclose a SASE. Unless [the query] is particularly captivating, if there's no SASE it goes into the wastebasket. And don't paper clip the stamps to the envelope. They can get lost that way—and it's better if you do the licking yourself."

THE ELEMENTS OF A QUERY LETTER

Although there are four main approaches you can take with formulating your query letter (and we will cover all of them), all query letters should contain the following elements:

> the hook
> the handle
> a mini-synopsis
> your credentials
> your credits
> what you're offering
> the closing

Let's look at each required element individually.

The Hook

Ideally, every novel should have a hook: a special plot detail or unique approach, a twist that grabs the readers' attention and makes them want to read more. It can be something that will make them say "ooh" when they hear it (more on eliciting the "ooh factor" in chapter four). A hook is a concept, an intriguing idea that readers would find compelling.

And if your novel has that hook, it must be evident in your query letter. If you can't identify that hook, it probably means you didn't build it in when you sat down to write your novel. It could be time to go back to the "plotting board" to rectify matters.

In Blythe's query letter for her novel *Parker's Angel* (provided as a sample later in this chapter) she reveals the hook in the first line of paragraph three: "Unlucky in love, Parker Ann Bell wouldn't recognize an angel if she pulled one back to earth with her—which is exactly what happens." Ooh.

In that one line we know what to expect from the book: romance and angels. It's a matter of taste if the topic interests you or not, but making your hook clear will help the agent or editor know right away if it's something for them.

The Handle

While the hook grabs the readers (i.e., agents or editors), the handle gives them something to hold onto. In other words, it's something they can use to determine if it's a book project they can sell.

To provide a handle you can identify your novel's theme—e.g., unrequited love, domestic violence, race relations—and also compare your book to something that's already out there. Agent Nancy Yost wants to learn from your query letter what kind of book it is and see a comparison of your book to similar titles. "The latter piece of information always helps because it tells me they know what's out there and they're current."

Agent Peter Rubie says, "Write what you want to write and how you want to write it. And then sit down at that point and decide 'How can I make what I have done commercial?' " When you've done that, you've provided a handle.

It could be in part identifying who your audience is. But this is another tricky part. Sometimes the audience is obvious. You don't have to go digging up statistics to tell romance editors that romance readers are female and between the ages of eighteen and ninety-eight. They already know all that. But, if you have written a book with a particular topic or theme that would be of interest to a particular segment of the population, then you should, indeed, mention it.

Anne Kinsman Fisher is the author of two novels: *The Legend of Tommy Morris* (Amber-Allen Publishing) and *The Masters of the Spirit* (HarperSanFrancisco, a division of HarperCollins). She hit the ground running, getting an acceptance within forty-eight hours of contacting an editor. There are two things to which she attributes her success: tailoring the topic for a specific editor and providing that editor with a handle to sell the book.

"It is possible to write your book specifically for an editor so you know that you've got precisely what they want," Fisher says. "An author friend was submitting a golf book and he got rejected by HarperSanFrancisco. The editor told him, 'Gosh, while I like your book, it's not the spiritual golf novel I've always been looking for.'

"I thought, 'Good golly. An editor who's looking for something!' I came up with an idea based on her words 'spiritual golf novel.'" And she sold it, too.

But Fisher didn't stop with just coming up with the right topic. She helped give the editor—and everyone on the editorial board—a handle, so they felt convinced the book would sell in the bookstores.

"I include a special section in my query/proposal on market research," Fisher says. "I tell my editor who will buy the book, specific numbers for the marketplace (e.g., for my book, women golfers are a growing audience). I include relevant articles about the popularity of my genre. I explain which other books are like mine and what they have sold. So, when my editor goes to her editorial meeting, she is prepared. Most writers worry only about getting an editor to like their work. They forget that the book actually needs to sell off the bookstore shelves."

Agent Evan Marshall says, "I really want to hear how the writer feels the book fits the market. I want to know that he has targeted his book for a certain audience, that he's done his homework. I realize that's largely my job, but I think all that has to start with the writer much more than it used to. If they are readers and are writing what they love to read, then chances are they know that the niche exists. Often the easiest way is to compare what they're doing with what's out there—a Mary Higgins Clark type women-in-jeopardy [novel], for example. Or they could just say they're writing a historical romance or a techno-thriller."

A Mini-Synopsis
In the synopsis part of your query you'll give an overview of your plot and introduce your main characters and their core conflict. Include a few plot high points, make the setting and time period clear and you're done.

Sound easy?

It isn't. Many successful authors will tell you that writing the novel was a lot easier than composing a query or a synopsis. In chapter six we cover synopsis writing in depth, and you'll get lots of helpful tips for making the synopsis section of your query letter effective.

In the meantime, just remember to not get too detailed—you can't put a complete blow by blow in two to four paragraphs. On the other hand, don't be so vague that the reader has no idea what you're hinting at.

Don't, for example, say, "Heroine X battles a multitude of problems before she solves the biggest one of all." This sentence includes what we call "empty phrases" and offers no information at all.

Do say, "Heroine X must cope with the abandonment by her husband, and a crooked judge hell-bent on revenge, before she can be reunited with the child he abducted." This version gives us a much better picture of what your book is about—and that's the sole purpose of the query letter's synopsis section.

Your Credentials

The purpose of the credentials section of your query letter is to convey knowledge of your subject matter and to give a little information about yourself.

Give this aspect of your proposal some creative thought before you decide you don't have anything to say. No, by "creative" we're not suggesting you make things up. (Save that for the novel!) If you're a lawyer working on a legal thriller, tell them. Been coaching Little League for thirty years? Tell them that, too, but only if your novel concerns Little League.

Agents and editors want to know who you are and how you came to write this novel. Agent Julie Castiglia says, "It annoys me when people don't include any information about themselves—what was the motivation for the book? If they want to write a book about Russia, I want to know why. Why are they qualified? Why are they interested?"

When discussing who you are, it's important not to get carried away. "Do not include your life's story, unless it's pertinent to what you've written," editor Marjorie Braman says.

Credentials could also include membership in writers organizations, awards or contests won, attendance at writing seminars and workshops or completion of writing courses. But here's where you need to tread carefully. Some agents and editors don't put much stock in this sort of thing. Editor Michael Seidman says, "Telling me of the award you won from a contest is beside the point. I've judged too many of them to take them that seriously as validation. I don't think you should mention awards unless they are from professional peer organizations."

Omitting mention of your degree in creative writing might be the safest course, too. Some editors and agents will be gratified to hear it. Others will try not to hold it against you.

Under the credentials section of your query letter you can also mention any access to sources you have. Almost all fiction projects require some research. The plot may be pure fabrication, but details of setting, for example, had better be dead-on accurate. If your book is set in the Middle East and you lived there for several years, mention that. But if you have no experience in that part of the world, your book's setting will be a harder sell.

No matter what other credentials you have—and even if you can't think of a single relevant scrap of experience that might help you—your best credential, the only one you absolutely must have, is a good proposal sent to the right person. If you've got this one, you've got a chance. Don't let any supposed deficiency stop you.

Your Credits

If you're a brand-new writer just starting out, you might not have any credits. That's OK. Just don't bring attention to it in a negative way. Don't apologize or even mention it—that's a surefire way of pointing out your amateur status. Michael Seidman says, "If you don't mention any fiction credits in your query letter, I'll assume it is a first novel; that has no bearing on when I read it or how carefully." The recipient of your query letter will infer that this is your first novel, and most agents and editors won't hold it against you.

Some put more stock in credits, and this could just mean that those aren't the right people for you to be querying. Agent Martha Millard says she prefers to look at potential clients who have a track record with published books to their credit, but any kind of credit—including publication of short stories or nonfiction in national magazines—is a step in the right direction. "Anyone who wants to interest an agent in reading her or his work should mention publishing credits right at the beginning of the query letter. There have certainly been times I have taken on writers with no publishing credits. In fact, I'm handling one right now. But if I spent all my time reading query letters and manuscripts from people who want to be published, believe me, I wouldn't have time to do anything else. When I turn down a query letter, it is because of the writer's credits and how he/she phrases the letter. If the letter isn't well written, it gives me a good idea that the book isn't going to be any good, either."

There are plenty of others, though, who are more than open to new writers and always looking for fresh talent. So don't worry if you lack a string of credits. Your writing will speak for itself.

And if you do have credits? Now is the time for a little horn tooting. Don't be shy, but don't be Barnum and Bailey, either. State your truth simply and directly.

Let's look at which credits to include and which might not be worth mentioning or might even go against you.

Of course, if you have any fiction credits, mention them: "My short stories have appeared in [names of the magazines]."

Blythe had one student, though, who had a slew of fiction credits, but was embarrassed to mention where they had appeared—in a series of erotica magazines. No reason not to mention those—look at Anne Rice and the work she has produced under a variety of pen names. But if, for whatever reason, you feel too shy, then just say, "My short stories have appeared in a variety of magazines," and don't mention their titles.

If you have any nonfiction publication credits, say so. "Any writing experience at all is of interest," says agent Jane Chelius.

If all the topics of your published work are irrelevant to your novel, just avoid going into too much detail. It's enough to say you're published. Period.

But if your current work of fiction is set during the Civil War, for example, and you have also published nonfiction pieces on the same topic, then definitely get specific about that.

There might be a few credits *not* worth mentioning—a letter to the editor of your local newspaper, an essay posted on an on-line message board, an article for your high school yearbook.

The point of listing credits is to show you have a track record, others have found your work acceptable, you are a professional and you have had experience working with editors.

What You're Offering

Make sure you give the title of your book, its word count and the genre. To do that you'll need to know what category or kind of book you've written.

Basic categories of fiction include (in alphabetical order)

action/adventure

children's

espionage

erotic

experimental

fantasy

gay/lesbian/bisexual

historical

horror

humor

inspirational/religious/spiritual

military

mystery

romance

science fiction

suspense

thriller (political/legal/medical)

western

women's

young adult (YA)

Many of these categories also have subgenres. The broad category of romance, for instance, includes subgenres such as contemporary, sweet, historical and Regency. Within the thriller category you will find medical, political, techno- and legal thrillers. Mysteries cover a wide range, too—cozies, police procedurals and detective.

If you can't find yourself in any of these categories, you may have a mainstream or literary novel on your hands.

Defining *mainstream*, though, is no easy task. Agent Kathleen Anderson says mainstream novels are "books people like to read. However, *mainstream* can also refer to general women's fiction, for example. Mainstream women's fiction generally takes a contemporary subject and writes about domestic/romantic situations. But, in fact, mainstream is becoming an outdated concept. It really refers to a straightforward narrative with no poetic twists, and that is not finding a large audience these days."

Editor Elisa Wares says, "I dislike the word *mainstream* because you can't go into a bookstore and find a shelf for a noncategory book. So, I would say mainstream is a book that doesn't fit into a category. Unless it is a best-seller (Grisham or King), a writer should try to find a category that can be shelved. I decide what category goes on the spines of all my books. If I think it has a greater or 'breakout' audience than a specific genre would have, I will put *fiction* on the spine."

When looking at the difference between category romance and mainstream romance, agent Evan Marshall says, "Category romance deals with slighter issues, and most important, centers completely on the developing romance between the man and the woman. Mainstream romance has many other things going on in the story, other subplots and issues—and these issues are bigger, more momentous. It boils down to weightiness of story."

Literary fiction is identified by the style of writing—the deep tones and textures it contains—in addition to its subject matter.

If you don't know the genre or if you're just not sure, leave it out. It is not always necessary to state it, especially if there are too many crossovers. (Blythe, for example, considers her novel *Parker's Angel* to fall into the mainstream/romantic/suspense/comedy/women's fiction genre with a hint of New Age—but she wouldn't tell an agent or editor that.) In the handle section of your query letter, comparing your book to another author's can be sufficient to categorize it.

The Closing

At the end of the query letter you offer to send more—the complete manuscript for a novel. Do not offer a choice. Do not offer to send sample chapters *or* the complete manuscript. Offer only the completed manuscript. (You shouldn't be querying if your manuscript isn't complete.) If they want to see more, they will tell you. They will also tell you what to send—sample chapters or the complete manuscript and a synopsis. You'll find information on how to prepare your proposal packet in part two of this book.

In closing your letter, less is more. Simply say, "May I send you the complete manuscript?" If you haven't made the title, genre and word count clear earlier, you can say instead, "May I send you my completed 100,000-word mainstream novel [title]?"

Titles, by the way, should be typed in italics (or underlined if you don't have an italic typeface) in your query letters. Don't use quotation marks or all caps.

There is no need to thank the editors and agents for their time and consideration or tell them you'll wait for their response or that you eagerly look forward to hearing from them. They know that, and such sentiments just take up room.

Additional elements that are not crucial but important to include in your query if available are:

- reason for selecting them
- referrals
- endorsements

Here is an explanation for each.

Reasons for Selecting an Editor or Agent

The process of selection seems pretty one-sided at this point. You're approaching the gatekeeper, proposal in hand, seeking admission into the select company of the published novelists.

But you had some reason for approaching this particular gatekeeper. It may help you to tell them what it is. A good reason may indicate a great deal about your preparation and your professionalism. If you have trouble coming up with a good reason, think back to the process when you first went through lists of agents and publishers, trying to find a good home for your masterpiece.

Bad reasons include:

- "You were one of the first ten agents, alphabetically, in the directory I used."
- "I've already approached 473 agents, and I finally got to you."
- "My mother's maiden name was Durning, just like yours, and I thought that might be lucky."

Good reasons include:

- A book you believe has special merit was represented by the agent or edited by the editor you're approaching.
- A book you believe has notable similarities to your project was handled by the agent or editor.

Referrals

Many agents aren't open to new clients unless they're referred by someone the agents know. Even if an agent is open to new writers, a referral can work wonders. Through all your networking at conferences, you may have met a lot of other writers by now. If one suggests you contact her agent, then by all means mention that up front in your query letter.

Even if you approach editors directly without an agent and you know one of their writers, mention it. No one likes to feel they're contacted blindly. In this situation—as long as it's true—name-dropping is an acceptable and helpful practice.

But keep in mind, knowing a successful, even a famous, writer might get your manuscript looked at more quickly, even more seriously, but nothing can guarantee you publication. It's all in your writing and how you present it.

Endorsements

You have to try to help your agent sell your work. Agent Peter Rubie says, "If I can turn around to an editor and say, 'Look, I've got this first-time writer who has a promise of a quote from John Le Carre.'"

Wouldn't that be wonderful? How do you go about getting such a quote? Well, you could be brazen and just send your manuscript off to your favorite best-selling author. Some of them might actually read it and answer.

Or you can canvas for a referral. "Most of the people who get published have gone through the trenches," Peter Rubie explains. "They've studied; they've done their homework; they've written; they've attended conferences and seminars. A lot of well-known writers teach or speak at these meetings. You can contact universities or the different writers groups and take the classes. This is how you make contacts."

Who knows, maybe Stephen King will endorse your horror novel with "This is even better than Dean Koontz!"

That's the stuff of which cover blurbs are made, a publisher's dream come true. (For agents, writers and booksellers, too!)

QUERY LETTER APPROACHES

There are four approaches you can use for the opening of your query:
1. The Formal Start
2. The Summary Statement

3. The Hook Start
4. The I've-Got-Connections Opening

Let's look at an explanation along with at least one sample letter for each category.

Approach #1: The Formal Start

In this approach you mention at the start that you are seeking representation or publication for your book, and you give its vital statistics (word count, genre, title) right up front. It is a formal approach that won't hurt you—but it also can be boring.

Although the sample query below is a very good letter, finding a more compelling opening might help the writer get even more positive responses than she has already received. Because she is sending it to an agent, it is obvious she is seeking representation. A better start would be with the second sentence, which is a good summary statement. The title could also be included there.

Note that all your query letters should address a specific editor or agent by name.

FORMAL START SAMPLE QUERY

February 17, 1999

Mr. John Smith
John Smith Literary Agency
1234 Main St., Suite 5
New York, NY 10001

Dear Mr. Smith:
I am currently seeking an agent for my completed 114,000-word historical romance *Tempting Fate*. The novel is set in 1851 Victorian England and focuses on two prominent families whose lives are

continued on next page

reunited in the heroine's fight to save orphans from factory labor.

The story opens as the resourceful Lady Alanna Clayton sets out to save a youth from being bonded to a worsted mill. Little does she realize that her seemingly benevolent act will thrust her into the arms of the one man whose memory has occupied a corner of her heart since she was thirteen years old.

When the dauntless Marquess of Aldwich, in need of an heir to save the family estate from his rapacious cousin, the Viscount Dormoth, catches Lady Alanna spiriting away a child from the almshouse, he uses the opportunity to blackmail her into marriage. The Marquess makes it very clear to Lady Alanna that the union will be for the sole purpose of providing a son. The very least he expects is to fall in love with her.

Throughout their escapades with the vengeful Viscount, Lady Alanna fights to win the devotion of the Marquess, while he struggles to repress his feelings, fearful of destroying the one woman who has ever loved him so unconditionally.

I am an active member of the national Romance Writers of America and our local Chicago-North chapter. This work, as well as two of my other historical romances, have won or placed in the following contests: the 1992 River City RWA Showdown Contest, the 1993 North Texas RWA Great Expectations Contest and the 1994 Monterey Bay Chapter Silver Heart Contest. Most recently, I learned *Tempting Fate* is a finalist in the Long Historical category of the 1997 National RWA Golden Heart Contest.

I have an article in the Spring/Summer 1997 issue of "The Wedding Pages" of *Chicago* magazine.

May I send you the complete manuscript?

Sincerely,

Michelle J. Hoppe

Approach #2: The Summary Statement

The summary statement approach begins with a sentence or two that gives an overall sketch of the book's plot, theme or setting. In essence, this approach provides the reader with the handle right up front.

SUMMARY STATEMENT SAMPLE QUERY #1

February 17, 1999

Mr. John Smith
John Smith Literary Agency
1234 Main St., Suite 5
New York, NY 10001

Dear Mr. Smith:

It's 1860 and the California-Oregon border seethes with racial hatred and greed. Whites and Indians butcher each other over the rich lands of the Lost River Valley. Despite this, Toby Winema-Riddle, a young Modoc woman, marries outside her race and challenges the male-dominated foundations of both white and Modoc societies. Sharing her true story are the two most important men in her life—her husband, Frank, and her cousin Kentapoos (known to history as "Captain Jack").

Winema yearns for peace, but battles her inbred need for revenge against raiding tribes and the casual brutality of local whites. Frank struggles to be accepted by the Modocs, but is often frustrated by an enigmatic line he cannot cross as a white man. Kentapoos's friendship with whites often conflicts with his Modoc roots and his ambition to become principal chief.

By 1864, Manifest Destiny and the overpowering resources of the whites force the Modocs to cede their lands. Life on the reservation becomes impossible for Kentapoos and his followers. His revolt ignites a tragic series of events that test Winema's spirit and courage, tear families apart and pull all of them toward a tragic and bitter vortex.

War with the U.S. Army erupts then quickly grinds to a stand-

continued on next page

still. A peace commission is appointed and offers Winema a mission—convince Captain Jack to surrender. If she cannot, her cousin and more than one hundred of her friends and family may die. Knowing she may lose her own life in the process, but emboldened by a prophetic vision, Winema makes a final heroic effort to change her cousin's mind.

But the level of mistrust on both sides is just too high. Politics and fear lead to assassination, betrayal, execution and exile. Yet, in the end, there are the promising seeds of a new generation and the blossoming of her foretold destiny as a peacemaker.

Lost River is a 90,000-word manuscript based on Winema's life. My research indicates this is the first novel ever written about Winema and her efforts to prevent the Modoc War of 1873. I have carefully researched the book, including interviews with direct descendants of the main characters. This is neither an Indian romance nor a western. It is an introspective portrayal of a Native American woman struggling to grapple with the grim realities of a changing world. To her anguish, she sees both sides. It would be easier if she could not. Would you be interested in seeing the complete manuscript?

I have had a short story and poetry published in *The Licking River Review*, *The Beaver Tail Journal* and *News From Indian Country* (a national Indian newspaper). *S.A.I.L. Magazine* (Studies in American Indian Literatures) published one of my book reviews. Two of my freelance business-related articles have been published in *Government Computer News* and *Restaurant News*.

Until my relocation to Connecticut in January 1997, I served as Vice President of The Butler County Council for Native Americans, located in Middletown, Ohio. I hold a degree in American History. I am a member of the Wordcraft Circle of Native Writers & Storytellers, and I am a "men's traditional" powwow dancer.

Respectfully,

Paxton Riddle

February 17, 1999

Mr. John Smith
John Smith Literary Agency
1234 Main St., Suite 5
New York, NY 10001

Dear Mr. Smith:

My historical romance, *Fiery Surrender*, tells the story of Monique von Strade—the headstrong daughter of a Prussian count—who knows from the moment she meets the enigmatic Pierre Latier that he would steal her heart as surely as he saved her honor. But love is the furthest thing from Pierre's mind. He's a man with a dark past who, under the guise of Pierre Marchant, serves King Louis XVI as a spy. Pierre can ill afford to think of anything save his upcoming mission of escorting French arms to the American Colonies.

When Pierre pays a sudden visit to her in Paris, Monique realizes the depth of the love she holds for him. Confessing her unwilling betrothal to a count she despises, she agrees to meet Pierre secretly. Within Pierre's passionate embrace, Monique can no longer deny the fierce, burning desires that flood her. Later, believing Pierre married her only to protect her family's honor, she resolves to win his love, even though it means following Pierre head-on into the dangers of war.

Set against the American Revolution and the October 1781 Battle of Yorktown, Virginia, *Fiery Surrender* is a sensual story of two people who eventually face the inevitability of their love. The novel runs approximately 130,000 words and is ready for an agent's assessment. To give authenticity to my novel, I have conducted considerable research at the Library of Congress and in both Williamsburg and Yorktown, Virginia.

I have an extensive background as an editor/creative writer and am an avid reader of historical and contemporary romances. I am an active

continued on next page

SUMMARY STATEMENT SAMPLE QUERY #2 (continued)

member of Washington Romance Writers, Virginia Romance Writers and Romance Writers of America. I am currently in the final stages of completing a second novel, a category mystery romance.

If the premise of the book appeals to you, I'd be happy to send the complete manuscript.

Sincerely,

Linda B. Morelli

SUMMARY STATEMENT SAMPLE QUERY #3

July 8, 2000

Ms. Samantha Simpson
Printed Passions, Inc.
1234 Main St.
New York, NY 10001

Dear Ms. Simpson:

Anticipation tingles up and down her spine. Her palms are sweaty and her heartbeat is unsteady. Computer analyst Sabrina Marshall shifts restlessly, waiting for Matthew Ross's turn at the podium. His reputation as a computer whiz is nationwide. His work is brilliant. His conference presentation is inspirational. Then she meets him. Oh, the charm! But Sabrina doesn't trust him. His lifestyle lacks commitment and his manner lacks sincerity.

Yet, those green eyes and that muscular body don't escape Sabrina's notice. Despite his coolness towards her, Sabrina is strongly attracted to him. She is surprised when he shows up in Washington, DC, as the new consultant—particularly when he acts as though they've never met!

Why is he so mysterious? His irregular work habits and traveling lifestyle have to be a cover-up. But for what? Convinced he really cares

continued on next page

for her, Sabrina gives him the benefit of the doubt. Until a problem is discovered—computer fraud. The evidence points to Matt. Angry and betrayed, Sabrina conducts her own investigation. She is determined to prove his guilt. Or is she?

My novel, *A Matter of Control*, a contemporary romance, runs approximately 58,000 words and is ready for submission. My five years as a computer programmer in the Washington, DC, area provided me with the experience for the background details used in this book.

May I send you the complete manuscript?
Sincerely,
Cynthia A. Scott

Approach #3: The Hook Start

Other queries jump right into the plot's action, starting with a good, attention-grabbing sentence. The first two or three paragraphs provide a mini-synopsis of your novel's plot. The next section highlights your credentials and credits, what you're offering and your closing. This opening works very well, especially if you don't know the person you are approaching.

HOOK START SAMPLE QUERY #1

February 17, 1999

Ms. Kelly Jones
Running Horse Books
1234 Main St.
New York, NY 10001

Dear Ms. Jones:

How would you feel, knowing the only man you ever loved needed you? Never mind that you haven't seen him for ten years, ever since

continued on next page

he betrayed you with another woman. Never mind that you had his child in secret, a daughter he never knew, a bright ray of sunshine whose existence on this earth was tragically cut short.

When Hope Glidewell left Dalhart, Texas, ten years ago, she'd vowed to have nothing further to do with Jeff Riggs, her high school sweetheart and the man who'd broken her heart. She'd kept her promise too, planning a full life for herself and her daughter, the child born of that deep, abiding love—a child who contracted leukemia and died before she'd ever had a chance to live, shattering Hope's world and changing her entire outlook on life.

Returning Home opens with Hope's arrival back in Dalhart. Jeff's mother has asked her to help. Jeff has been injured in a robbery, and while physically he has recovered, his memory has disturbing blanks. Because she has never forgotten Jeff, Hope is unable to resist returning home to see him one more time.

The trials both will face as Jeff regains his memory are difficult—for Hope must learn not only to forgive Jeff, but to forgive herself. And when Jeff learns of the brief existence of a daughter he never knew, will his love for Hope be enough to overcome the devastating betrayal?

Returning Home is completed, roughly 60,000 words. I am a published author—*Desert Fire* was an October 1997 release from Kensington Precious Gems and *Diamond in the Rough* was released in May 1998. I was also first runner-up in Silhouette's Shadows contest (out of more than six hundred entries). I would be more than happy to send you the entire manuscript upon your request.

Sincerely,

Karen Whiddon

February 17, 1999

Mr. John Smith
John Smith Literary Agency
1234 Main St., Suite 5
New York, NY 10001

Dear Mr. Smith:

Kidnapped, then buried alive by white slavers, Celeste Bates escapes into the arms of Captain Brent MacGraft, who mistakes her for his assassin. That fated night in 1857, Brent MacGraft expects an attempt on his life. What he doesn't expect is Celeste Bates. When she steals on board his ship in London bound for Wilmington, North Carolina, Celeste doesn't know the price for her freedom will be her heart.

Finding themselves entangled within the web of black-hearted white slaver Morgan Gaust's obsession and insatiable need for revenge, Celeste and Brent catapult into a conspiracy of betrayal. To unravel it, they must overcome their mistrust of each other. Their impromptu drunken wedding only reinforces Celeste's misgivings. Convinced her marriage to Brent is a farce, she flees. In a desperate attempt to resume her life, Celeste careens headlong into the arms of an unwanted fiancé, prearranged by her unsuspecting family.

When Brent marries Celeste, it is forever. His relentless pursuit of her and determination to bring Morgan to justice forces Celeste to face her fears. In the end, she must embrace her true feelings for Brent and offer her life to save his or be lost forever within the *Shadows of Love*.

Experienced as a professional copywriter, I am also published in nonfiction, including contributing writer-editor of a second edition historical booklet and several newsletters. In addition, I am a recent finalist in two RWA chapter contests: the Opening Gambit 1996 Writing Competition and the 1996 Golden Synopsis. I am a member of RWA, Carolina Romance Writers Chapter, the North Carolina

continued on next page

Writers Network and Writers Club Romance Group.

Should *Shadows of Love* interest you, the completed manuscript of 100,000 words and a synopsis are available upon request. For your convenience, I have enclosed an SASE.

Sincerely,

Sally Painter Kale

February 17, 1999

Ms. Kelly Jones
Running Horse Books
1234 Main St.
New York, NY 10001

Dear Ms. Jones:

What if a New York-based, love-starved Jewish immigrant were flying to Mexico to smuggle his pen pal into the U.S.? And what if he and his girl got robbed on the beach in Acapulco and were left behind naked? My novel, *Lie Under the Fig Trees*, shows how the survivors moved from shock and loss to celebration of life, even though less than perfect.

Today's readers have shown they want books that are both suspenseful and topical. Mexico has been and will remain very much in the nightly news as well as a travel paradise for years to come. My story shows readers what happens in the shadows of ritzy beachfront hotels. I have thoroughly researched the background, including the incident in Acapulco, where I was a victim of an attack myself.

The manuscript runs 50,000 words and is currently ready for submission. I have made the transition into the English language since my arrival in the U.S. in 1977, and I have taught creative writing at Hartnell College since 1992. My work has appeared in *The*

continued on next page

Baltimore Sun, The Hemingway Review and a dozen little literary magazines.

I enclose a synopsis of *Lie Under the Fig Trees*, along with a SASE for your convenience.

May I send you my complete manuscript?

Sincerely,

Tad Wojnicki

Approach #4: The I've-Got-Connections Opening

You can take this approach if you already know the person you are contacting—maybe you met at a conference—another writer is referring you or you're already a well-published writer, perhaps seeking a new agent or publishing house. (In this instance most agents and editors recommend a phone call as the most direct route, but if you're not comfortable with the phone, this would be the way to go.)

In this approach you'd mention right up front how you happened to be contacting this particular agent or editor and include your relevant credits, then go on to summarize the book you're offering.

In the following sample letter (see pp. 72-73), notice how Blythe starts with her connection, then provides a handle for the book by comparing it to something similar, offers the theme and then the hook at the start of the summary paragraphs.

BUILDING KILLER QUERY LETTERS

Now that you've seen some effective sample query letters, it's time to sit down and actually compose one. For some this might seem like a daunting task; writing the novel was so much easier. But it doesn't have to be difficult. Look at it as a writing exercise. Compose your first draft, put it aside for awhile, then come back to it with fresh eyes. For your second read, replace your writer's cap with an editor's one and look for and correct any trouble spots.

February 17, 1999

Mr. John Smith
John Smith Literary Agency
1234 Main St., Suite 5
New York, NY 10001

Dear Mr. Smith:

Last year your interview appeared in *Fiction Writer's Guideline*, the newsletter I put out for Fiction Writer's Connection. You mentioned you were open to submissions from FWC members, and I hope that applies to the director as well.

I am seeking representation for my 93,000-word novel, *Parker's Angel*, a mainstream romantic comedy in a similar vein to the movie *Ghost*. It takes a tongue-in-cheek look at near-death experiences and America's ongoing fascination with angels. With a whimsical Beatles motif running throughout, it's also the story of a young woman who must learn to trust and love again.

Unlucky in love, Parker Ann Bell wouldn't recognize an angel if she pulled one back to earth with her—which is exactly what happens. During the renovations of her new bookstore, Parker is electrocuted trying to help a workman in trouble. It takes her a few moments to understand why she's floating inches from the ceiling, her own body lying on the floor beneath her. She views the bright light, the tunnel and the faceless angel at the end of it with a healthy skepticism, but after she is brought back to life, a series of events becomes impossible to explain away in earthly terms.

She studies each new person she meets for signs of an otherworldly nature—the Hemingway look-alike who is the proprietor of the bookstore next to hers; her new suitor, Desmond; and Molly Jones, her recently hired assistant. But Parker doesn't really believe angels exist. She tries to convince herself her near-death experience was a dream or the result of a brain starved for oxygen.

continued on next page

Desmond doesn't help matters; he keeps insisting he's an angel who has loved Parker from afar. A little bit of mind reading, blue lights flashing whenever Desmond kisses her, events mimicking the lyrics of a Beatles song ("Obla di, Obla da, life goes on . . ."), surfacing memories of a previous near-death experience, and miraculously healing of injuries received during an attack all push Parker toward believing. Parker falls in love with Desmond, but by then it's too late—he has to return to his heavenly duties. Is there another angel in Parker's life who can put everything right? She finds out there is.

I am a full-time writer with thirty-eight nonfiction books to my credit. I am also director of Fiction Writer's Connection, and I teach a "How to Approach Editors and Agents" course on America Online. Two other unpublished novels (both women in jeopardy) have been optioned for movies.

May I send you the complete manuscript for *Parker's Angel*?

Regards,

Blythe Camenson

QUERY LETTER CHECKLIST

Here's a checklist of items to watch for and fix.

____ Weak lead sentence

____ Wordiness

____ Awkward phrasings

____ Lack of clarity

____ Illogical paragraph organization

____ Repetitiveness

____ Weak verbs

____ Clichés

____ Lack of rhythm

____ Overusing adjectives and adverbs

Eleven Query Letter Tips

1. The style in your query should reflect the style of the project you are proposing.

2. Make sure you state your novel's word count. This is important information in deciding how to market your book—and if it can be marketed. Editor Michael Seidman points out that he absolutely needs to know word count. "At Walker & Company I'm stuck with very strict length guidelines—70,000 words—so it helps me to know what I'm dealing with. If the length is just slightly over or under, it's workable, but with something like a 97,000-word manuscript, I'd say no right from the git-go and not waste my time or yours."

3. Don't say you write like a particular best-selling writer. You should just say you write in the same genre as that author or in a style similar to hers. It's a fine distinction, but knowing the difference can prevent your annoying some editors and agents.

4. Avoid mentioning how many people have read and loved your book. The opinions of Aunt Mary and Uncle Fred won't help build your case. The agents and editors would prefer to decide for themselves.

5. Stay clear of self-glorifying adjectives (save those for the book reviewers). Don't give into the temptation of describing your work as dazzling, dramatic, exciting, fast-paced or anything else. Say, "My book is an account of . . .," not "My book is a fascinating account of. . . ."

   "I have a letter from someone that said something to the effect that 'I am the next major literary writer of my generation. You cannot afford to not read my book," agent Peter Rubie says. "I sent him a standard rejection slip, but my personal reaction was 'This is absurd.' If you're not published yet, you're not the best

continued on next page

judge of your own material. I represent some very solid writers—they've won awards and have achieved a lot—but they don't come across like that, even though they're far closer to that level."

6. Avoid predicting your book's climb up the best-seller lists (no one can predict that). "It's a good idea not to mention in your letter that you think your novel is going to be Avon's next best-seller," editor Marjorie Braman says. "Publishers are never sure about that. I don't know how an author can be sure."

The grander the brag and boast, the bigger the turnoff.

7. Propose only one project in a single query. You can mention that you have other books in the works (if you do), but don't go into too much detail on those in this particular query letter. Agents and editors want to know you're not a one-book wonder, but don't cloud the waters with too many projects in one query letter.

If you are writing a series, say so, but your query should propose book one. Sending out a query for book two before book one has been accepted tells agents and editors that the first book didn't fly. "If you are submitting the third novel in a series to me, I'd like to know that there were two before it," notes agent Richard Henshaw. "I'd also like to know what your plans are down the road."

In fact, this information may be the most important thing you can say. "I like to handle an author for their career, not by the book," Henshaw says. "If I liked the writing of this particular project but didn't find it commercial enough to take on, a good pitch on the next project might encourage me to ask for a look when it's ready."

8. Don't put yourself down in a query letter. Ever. Don't say it's your first book or you hope they'll like it. Of course, it is; of course, you do.

continued on next page

9. Don't tell the editor or agent his business. While you need to be market savvy and show you know the market for your book, there's a fine line to walk here. Michael Seidman says, "Nothing gets me angrier than seeing something like "Female PIs are selling big, so you'll love my book." Your impression of the market is based on what's there now, not on the sales we're seeing or the comments we get from wholesalers and jobbers." Just state what your book is about, what niche it falls into, but unless you have actual current sales statistics at hand, don't dig a hole for yourself.

10. Be nice. Don't discuss the advance you envision, the rights you are prepared to offer or any demands of any sort. Nothing will turn off an editor or agent faster than a show of arrogance. "You'd be amazed at how many query letters I receive that are out-and-out rude," agent Nancy Yost says.

11. Don't show your desperation. You've written ten previous novels, all unpublished. You have completely rewritten this one three times. You have polished it twenty. And if this one doesn't fly, your plan is to chuck writing forever and find the nearest bridge, nunnery or French Foreign Legion recruitment office. This is information that no agent or editor wants to know; it can only undermine your efforts. ▲

_____ No transitions (or weak ones) between paragraphs
_____ Weak plotting (as related in the query)
_____ Incorrect punctuation, grammar and spelling

What follows are two drafts for a query letter written by a new author. The first draft is the original. With the above checklist in mind, read through it and see how many problem areas you can find. Then go on to the final, polished draft. Our comments point out what works and why we think so.

February 17, 2000

Mr. John Smith
John Smith Literary Agency
1234 Main St., Suite 5
New York, NY 10001

Dear Mr. Smith,

Perhaps no other musical oeuvre has inspired as much passion worldwide, in aristocrats and commoners alike, as that of Beethoven. In my mainstream novel, *Chords of Fire*, Beethoven's music drives the protagonist as if it ❶ were a character itself.

Those who love this music often find in it an almost religious "meaning." ❷ Hearing Beethoven's Seventh Symphony at the age of sixteen gave Adam Faulke, an ordinary teenager and a lousy cellist, his first taste of religious majesty. This experience set him in motion and changed his life. ❸

At the opening of *Chords of Fire*, Adam, now an accomplished musician, is the principal cellist of the Philadelphia Orchestra. The book's first mystery ❹ begins to unfold at the orchestra's gala opening concert, when, to Adam's great dismay, he passes out while the orchestra is playing to an audience of three thousand people. Of all things, they are playing Beethoven's Seventh Symphony.

To his friends, he says, "It was the heat." But it wasn't the heat, any more than it was the position of the moon or what he had ❺ for dinner. It was the first in a series of unfathomable occurrences which

continued on next page

1. Not clear what the *it* refers to. The way this is constructed, *it* refers to the protagonist.
2. Do not put *meaning* in quotes.
3. The opening line of the query leads us to think the novel is about Beethoven. Here we see it isn't. The writer needs to be clear right up front who this is about.
4. Although mainstream novels can have an element of mystery to them, this might make the reader think this is a mystery novel.
5. Should be "what he'd had."

plunge Adam into a growing confusion, one which ❻ threatens to derail his fledgling solo career and to sabotage his previously placid life. ❼

After the opening night debacle, Adam begins to have odd dreams, dreams ❽ in which he is playing a piece of unknown but intricate music on an old piano. From chapter sixteen, "The Ghost Music": "Before long the mad music dream came, with more delirious impact than ever before. My fingers bored into the piano, milking bewitchment from its innards. My hands ranged crazily over the keys, drawing ghostly wails and howls of protest. Not music, but a pact with God, or maybe the devil." ❾

Chords of Fire, while not New Age fiction, shares with *The Celestine Prophecy* a quest for ageless spiritual "truths" which ❿ transcend the banality of everyday life. ⓫

The protagonist's eventual realizations speak to a creeping ennui, one from which many people today are awakening with the question, "But isn't there something more?"

Chords of Fire is a story of urgency, friendship, and love. And ultimately, it is a story of discovery—of one's own purpose, of what it is to be an artist and of what it is to be human. By the story's end, Adam answers his burning questions, and the answers set him free.

May I send you the completed manuscript?

Sincerely,

Julie Goldman Connard

---

6. Both "whichs" in sentence should be "that," not "which."
7. Repetitive. The point about the "first mystery" has already been made. We need more meat, fewer hints.
8. Second *dreams* is repetitive. In addition, *opening* has been used three times.
9. Not clear that writer is quoting her own work. Delete excerpt.
10. Which should be that.
11. More genre confusion: It isn't New Age, yet the writer compares it to a New Age novel. Previously she called it mainstream, then threw in mysteries. The best bet is to let the agent decide for himself.

Although we get a sense that this query speaks for a compelling, literate book, we'd like to know more about what the protagonist's conflict is—what it is that will hook us and keep us reading.

We are more confused than intrigued, and we want to be intrigued. We want to say, "Ooh, this is a book to read." But right now, there's no grit to sink our teeth into. Why does Adam pass out—what is happening to him? If we knew that we'd probably want to read this book. We want an idea of what to expect. The writer is teasing too much.

In addition, the query is too long.

This query letter went through several more drafts before reaching this final version. In the final draft, our editorial comments point out what works and why.

FINAL DRAFT OF QUERY LETTER FOR *CHORDS OF FIRE*

February 17, 2000

Mr. John Smith
John Smith Literary Agency
1234 Main St., Suite 5
New York, NY 10001

Dear Mr. Smith:

In my mainstream novel, *Chords of Fire*, Beethoven's music drives the protagonist, cellist Adam Faulke, as if the music were a character itself. ❶

Those who love this music often find in it an almost religious meaning. Hearing Beethoven's Seventh Symphony at the age of sixteen gave Adam, an ordinary teenager and a lousy cellist, his first taste of religious majesty. This experience catalyzed his reach for musical excellence. ❷

At the beginning of *Chords of Fire*, Adam, now an accomplished performer, is the principal cellist of the Philadelphia Orchestra. The book's drama unfolds at the orchestra's gala opening concert, when,

continued on next page

1. This is a good, straightforward opening—much clearer than in the original draft.
2. Good characterization—"ordinary teenager and lousy cellist."

to Adam's great dismay, he passes out while the orchestra is playing to an audience of three thousand. Of all things, they are playing Beethoven's Seventh Symphony.

To his friends, he says, "It was the heat." But it wasn't the heat, any more than it was the position of the moon or what he'd had for dinner. It was the first in a series of occurrences that plunge Adam into a growing confusion, one that threatens to derail his fledgling solo career and to sabotage his previously placid life.

After the opening night debacle, Adam has an odd dream in which he is playing a piece of unknown but intricate music on an old piano. Adam's hands range madly over the instrument, "milking bewitchment from its innards." His fingers draw "ghostly wails and howls of protest."

He becomes obsessed with finding this music, which he begins to suspect is real. And find it he does—in Europe. These and other events lead Adam to conclude that he has lived before, in another time and place. But for Adam, acknowledging this thought is tantamount to admitting he's crazy. ❸

To resolve the confusion eroding his focus, his relationships and his love of making music, Adam must first confront those haunting traces from another life. By the story's end, Adam answers his questions about the past, and the answers set him free.

Chords of Fire shares with *The Celestine Prophecy* a quest for ageless spiritual truths that transcend the banality of everyday life. ❹

Adam's eventual realizations speak to a creeping ennui, one from which many people today are awakening with the question, "But isn't there something more?" Through music and the help of a woman, Adam learns that there is.

May I send you the completed manuscript?

Sincerely,

Julie Goldman Connard

---

3. Now we are getting a better sense of what the mysteries are that were only hinted at in the first draft.
4. The writer provides the agent with a good handle here.

BACK TO THE PLOTTING BOARD

Writing a good query letter can often be a revealing exercise. If it's proving to be overly troublesome—you can't seem to find the hook or identify your main character's conflict, for example—the problem might be a flawed plot. The hook or conflict just isn't in your novel to identify. This is a hard—but incredibly valuable—lesson to learn. It means putting the query letter aside and going back to the plotting board. A revised novel with a clear-cut hook and conflict will lend itself to a much easier query letter and will be much easier to sell.

SLOW AND STEADY OR THE BLITZ APPROACH?

Let's say your novel and query letter are finished and you're ready to get started hitting the marketplace. How many query letters to send out at a time is an important consideration. Say you have identified forty possible agents who handle the genre in which you're writing. Should you fire up the printer and mail your query to all forty at once? Probably not.

Say your manuscript gets rejected by all forty and you decide to do a rewrite. You may end up with a better book, but where will you send it now? You've already queried your top forty choices of agents, and chances are they aren't going to want to look at something they've already rejected. Your blitz has left you with no good options.

To avoid eliminating all potential agents or editors, start by sending out your query to five at a time. If feedback comes back with rejection letters, then you have the opportunity to revise and still have fresh avenues to which you can submit.

This brings us to a common question new writers ask: "But if I have revised the novel so completely that it's almost unrecognizable from its former self, and it's definitely so much better, and I have a new query letter to go along with it, why can't I query the same people again?"

Sometimes you can—with a completely revised book and query letter proposing it, the passage of time and a new title to boot, you might get away with it. (The new title is important—most agencies and major publishing houses log all submissions into their computer by author, date and title. If the same title were to come around again, it would show on the computer and you'd be found out.)

Not all agents will remember your first query letter. Agent Richard Henshaw says, "The truth is that I receive so many queries that if one didn't make an impression the first time around, in a month or so I'll probably be able to read it with a fresh eye. So, yes, I will reconsider queries, but there's a good chance I didn't pass on it because the query wasn't effective. It might just not be the sort of story I'm looking for at the moment."

Other agents have excellent memories and will remember a query letter they previously rejected. Unless an agent or editor has suggested (or implied) willingness to take a second look at a revised work, there's not much point in querying about a book to the same people again.

Simultaneous and Multiple Submissions

Sending a query out to more than one agent or editor at a time is called a *simultaneous submission*. This is often confused with a *multiple submission*, which means sending more than one project at a time to the same editor or agent.

In the midst of the slow and steady approach—or if one couldn't resist, the blitz approach—many new writers wonder if they should be announcing their simultaneous submission tactics to the agents and editors they are approaching. There are different schools of thought on this. Many agents and editors ask to be informed. They say it will spur them to get to your work faster if they know there's competition.

Others don't want to bother with simultaneous submissions; they don't want the pressure of the competition. Nor do they want to invest the time it takes to read your query, scribble a request for more across it, then stuff it into your SASE, only to learn later you've been snapped up by another agent or your book found a home at another publishing house.

Our feeling is this: Say you start writing a novel at age thirty-five, finish it at age thirty-seven. You send out one query letter, wait six weeks for a reply. Now let's say that reply is positive. You send in your manuscript and wait another three months for a reply. If that response is negative, you send out another query letter and start the process all over again. Now you're thirty-eight. By the time you approach the forty agents on your list, you'll be—what—53?

Unless you want to spend the rest of your life trying to sell your first novel (never mind the second or third or fourth), sending out simultaneous query letters is the only way to go—and we don't think there's any need to announce your approach tactics.

The rules differ for simultaneous submissions of manuscripts, though, and we've covered that topic for you in chapter five.

E-mail or "Snail Mail"?

Don't send your query to editors and agents via E-mail unless you are sure this form of communication is acceptable. Although more and more agents and some editors are willing to consider electronic submissions, many still reply the old-fashioned way. E-mail, by nature, invites a fast reply. This is great for positive responses, but it's very easy to make a snap decision and turn down an E-mail query.

Agent Richard Henshaw says, "I look at brief queries on-line, but that is really a screening-out process. If something definitely isn't right, it saves everyone postage."

In summary, you want to send a professional, strong, to-the-point query letter that avoids hype or gimmicks. A commercially viable idea presented concisely will get you requests for more.

In later chapters we'll show you how to compose, format and submit that "more," but first we'll tell you how to bypass the query letter step altogether.

CHAPTER
FOUR

THE PITCH

"An editor is a person who knows precisely what he wants, but isn't quite sure." —Walter Davenport

N ow that you've learned how to write a query letter, we'll show you how you can sometimes bypass that step and get right to a request to see your manuscript. This can happen at writers conferences, which feature, in addition to speakers and workshops, agents and editors who have come to share their knowledge and find new talent.

We discussed conferences in some detail in chapter two, but now it's time to focus in on that ten-, fifteen- or twenty-minute appointment. This is your chance to pitch your novel to an agent or editor face-to-face, find out if there is interest and—happily—forego the query letter stage—at least with these particular agents and editors.

If your idea is a hit, the agent or editor will ask you to send material—maybe sample chapters, maybe the whole manuscript— back to the office after the conference is over.

Do not bring your manuscript to the conference, though, with the expectation that agents or editors will read it on the spot or take it home with them. They will be meeting with a lot of writers and couldn't possibly carry all that material back on the plane. Don't worry, they won't forget you. (In part two, we show you how to prepare your solicited submission package, including the cover let- ter—which, among other things, serves as a reminder to the agent or editor of where you met.)

ARRANGING THE AGENT/EDITOR APPOINTMENT

For those of you who are new to writers conferences, you might be wondering how these talks with agents and editors get arranged. No, you don't have to sidle up to them at the bar or break through a crowd of schmoozers to schmooze yourself. (You certainly can try these approaches if you want—but never, *ever* interrupt them in the rest room!) Most conferences will give you an option on the registration form to sign up for an appointment. When you get to the conference, you will be told the time and place of your meeting.

Some conference sponsors will wait until the first day of the conference to put out sign-up sheets. In that case, it's a good idea to come early to make sure you can grab a slot with the agent or editor of your choice.

How many agents and editors you'll get to see will depend on the conference—and your assertiveness. Some might allow you only one official appointment. But that doesn't mean you won't get to talk to the others in attendance. Here's where the schmoozing comes in—in the hallway between talks, at the bar, during lunch or dinner, poolside, over a smoke outside.

Most conferences do not charge for the official appointment, but recently a few have started to—maybe $10 to $20 for each appointment you make. It is well worth the extra money. Indeed, it is well worth the conference fee just to get to meet an agent or editor face-to-face. Many writers find agents—even publishers—this way.

WHO CAN PITCH?

Anyone who has signed up for a conference and laid down the money is entitled to pitch to an agent or editor. But some agents and editors prefer your work be completed before taking up their time.

Agent George Nicholson says, "I love writers conferences that are beautifully organized. At conferences, I've met some wonderful writers who eventually became my clients. At one conference, though, a guy had an appointment to meet with me for twenty minutes. I read his submission, which was just awful. I asked him how long he had been writing for children and he said since last night. I had to laugh, but it was hard for me to take this guy seriously. He had paid his money, so he was entitled to his twenty minutes. It was very frustrating, because instead of spending that twenty minutes talking to a serious writer, I spent that time guiding him to the books he should be reading."

That's an extreme example. Most people don't decide the night before a conference they want to become writers. Many conference attendees are in the middle of a project and come to get feedback on their idea, to see if they are heading in the right direction—and that's perfectly legitimate. You can have an appointment even though your novel isn't completed. Just make sure you let the agent or editor know that. They can tell you if your project interests them, if the plot works for them. The feedback you might get could be invaluable for going home and revising and polishing your book. And when you're done, you know you have an interested party to approach. That knowledge can provide wonderful motivation for finishing the project and making it your best work ever.

BATTLING THE NERVES

That time has finally come—your appointment with an agent or editor. You are more nervous than you thought possible. Your mouth is dry. Your hands are clammy. You'd rather be anywhere but here.

OK, come on now. You need to relax about this. Agents and editors are just like any other people. Some of them you'll hit it off with. Some of them will help you feel comfortable. Some of them will not.

Agent Julie Castiglia says, "People shouldn't be intimidated by agents. It's just a job, like any other job. If you are a professional writer, you should have no fear of approaching an agent."

But you're probably not a professional writer, and you think you have every right to be nervous. You feel as if your whole writing future is at stake. (It isn't—there are tons of agents out there.) But if you're feeling so nervous you can hardly speak, try telling the agents or editors that. You might be surprised at how understanding they can be. Your confession might just break the ice.

Keep in mind why agents and editors are at this conference. They are not doing you a favor. They do not like flying any more than you do. They are looking for new stars—for the next John Grisham, Mary Higgins Clark or Stephen King. And you just might be that person. The agent is psychologically disposed toward liking you, toward liking your project. So is the editor. You've got the edge. You might be the next writer to hit the best-seller list.

Best-selling author Tom Clancy sums it up well: "What do you suppose editors do? They look for new talent. My editor was an editor when we started together. Now he's editor in chief and publisher. His replacement will get there by discovering new talent, too."

INTERVIEWING AGENTS

While you are worrying so much about the agents judging you, don't forget another reason you are there—to judge the agents. Yes, you will tell them about your project. But if the agents express interest, you can also use the time to find out how they work. Come prepared with questions of your own: Do they have any houses in mind where your book might fit? Do they make simultaneous submissions? Do they work with a contract? Ask whatever you need to know. You might decide that this is not an agent you want to send your work to, even if the agent does express interest. The conference appointment should be a give-and-take. It's a short period of time, granted, but both of you should be able to come away with something—the agent, a sense of your book; you, a sense of the agent.

BE PREPARED

Now that you have the appointment, what do you do? The best advice is to come prepared. Have a pitch ready. That means coming up in advance with a way to describe your story that will capture interest and avoid long-windedness.

Be prepared, also, for questions the agent or editor might ask you for further clarification. If you go on and on before you get to the point, the agent or editor will figure you do the same in your book. Although it's impossible to judge your writing from a verbal pitch, how you present your project during this face-to-face query will influence the way the agent or editor views your work.

So what happens during that short appointment? First of all, you will arrive on time. If you're late, don't demand that the "time monitor" squeeze you in. Also, you won't keep the agent over the allotted time. You probably will notice out of the corner of your eye a long line of other eager writers waiting for their turns.

You'll probably introduce yourself, shake hands, sit down across from each other and exchange business cards. Have your cards ready. You can also handwrite the name of your book on the back of the card as a reminder. Then the agent or editor might say, "How can I help you?" Here is where you get to pitch your novel.

THE ANATOMY OF A PITCH

You have only a few minutes—you want your pitch to make clear what type of book you're offering and what the theme or the plot line is—in general. You can't go into every plot detail here. You shouldn't.

Another thing you shouldn't do is brag shamelessly about your book. Most new writers are too nervous to even think to do that, but every once in a while, someone breaks that golden rule. Agent Rob Cohen has run across it often enough. "I don't like it when someone tells me their book is great," she says. "Some of the best writers I know think their own work is terrible."

A good place to start is to come up with a one-line pitch—a pitch line—to give an idea of your plot. Feel awkward just blurting out something that might sound like a movie poster or a book-jacket blurb? Then simply tell them you've prepared a pitch line. We're sure they'll ask to hear it.

What is a pitch line? A pitch line is a short, punchy, oral presentation of your plot. It must be short—it would be pretty difficult to memorize a three- or four-line pitch—and you must deliver it effectively.

The best pitch lines elicit the ooh factor. It makes the listeners say, "Ooh, I want to read that book."

What's another way to say "ooh factor?" It's the "hook," the angle. Hollywood types call it "the premise." We talked about the hook in chapter three. If you are working on a book that doesn't have a hook, you're going to have a difficult time describing your project—you are also going to have a difficult time *selling* your project. That hook must be in your pitch and in your query letter. If it isn't in your book, you can't get it anywhere else.

Make sure you have your hook established in your mind before you get too far into your book, or better yet, before you even start it. If you're having trouble coming up with a pitch line that elicits the ooh factor, it's a sign you need to go back to your novel's plot and create a hook that is more intriguing, more compelling. To sell your book it has to have an angle different from all the other books on the shelves. That's the first thing you need to come up with—an idea that *is* the hook.

The spoken pitch line can be jazzy, but it has to have the most important elements in it. What's most important to your plot? Conflict! Every novel needs conflict—your pitch should show the main problem your hero or heroine will face.

Here's one of our favorite pitches: "Recent law school grad is offered a job that seems too good to be true—and it is." Do you recognize that? Right. John Grisham's *The Firm*.

Here are a few other examples:
- "Young female FBI agent risks her life and resolves personal issues as she seeks help from imprisoned serial killer to catch another." (*The Silence of the Lambs*)
- "Writer is tortured by psychotic woman claiming to be his Number One Fan." (*Misery*)
- "Greedy man offers wife as vessel to bear child fathered by Satan." (*Rosemary's Baby*)

After the Delivery

Your pitch doesn't have to give the whole plot (although you'll probably discuss it more after you give your pitch line); you just have to give the agent or editor a handle on your book. During your appointment, just as you would in your query letter, you could also compare your book to something similar. This is another way the agent or editor can get a handle on your book.

Make sure you also tell them the title, the genre and the word count. The setting is important, too. Agent Kathleen Anderson says, "You should be sure, wherever possible, to be specific about setting in your pitches. Instead of a small town, say what town, where; instead of Africa, where in Africa."

Allow the agent time to ask you any questions. Try to make the conversation a give-and-take.

After the appointment is over, take a deep breath—you survived after all! Then make a quick note of what the agent or editor had to say. You might be meeting with several. You don't want to confuse what they asked to see or how they asked for your material to be submitted.

OTHER PITCH LINE USES

Conferences are not the only time to use your pitch line. There are actually other reasons to have one prepared:

1. Friends and family are probably always asking you what you're writing about. If their eyes start to glaze over when you tell them—well, you get the idea. Trying your pitch out on them is a good place to get some practice.

2. If your pitch is short enough, it can even be your query letter's first sentence. "In your letter state in one sentence what the book is about," says agent Susan Zeckendorf. "You have to catch the agent's eye right away."

3. If you already have an agent who is willing to discuss projects with you before you sit down to write, a pitch line will help you present your plot ideas for feedback.

Ten Tips for Attending Seminars and Conferences

1. Take plenty of business cards with you to exchange with other writers and speakers. When you get your cards printed up, avoid putting *writer* or *author* next to your name (it's viewed as pretentious), unless you are a professional freelancer looking for work.

2. Make a brief note on the back of each business card you receive as a memory jogger for later. After a full day or two of meeting new people, you might not be able to connect the name with the conversation you had.

3. Make an effort to introduce yourself to at least five new people. Most people attend conferences on their own and probably feel as shy and awkward as you do. You obviously have something in common—your love of writing—so for a good icebreaker, you can ask about the other person's specialty or area of interest.

4. Take a folder or tote bag with you to organize all the handouts you'll receive. Don't forget a notebook.

5. Pace yourself. Attend the sessions that interest you the most, but don't try to cram everything in. A chat with a new acquaintance over a cup of coffee in the lounge can be as informative as a string of seminar sessions, one after the other.

6. Ask permission before tape-recording any of the sessions. You might be infringing upon prior arrangements between the conference organizers and a commercial outfit taping the sessions for sale.

7. Wear comfortable shoes! You will be on your feet a lot. Dress comfortably, but appropriately. Writers conferences are not formal affairs, but you will be meeting agents and editors in a professional capacity, and you want to make a good impression.

continued on next page

8. If you've signed up for an agent/editor appointment, come prepared. Have your pitch ready and your questions written out in advance.

9. Follow through on the contacts you made. Pick up the phone or write a letter. The networking opportunities seminars offer are as important as the sessions.

10. Do not burn any bridges. You would be surprised how many writers break that golden rule. There are always stories circulating. (A writer lost a contest, then verbally attacked the judge—in the rest room. An agent was not interested in the writer's manuscript, so the writer began berating her for her lack of intelligence and foresight.) The writing community is small. You don't want to become known for your lack of professionalism.

As we mentioned earlier, developing a good pitch line helps you to define the focus of your book for yourself. Whether your novel is still in the planning stages or already filling up two or three floppy disks, it's a good idea to have ready a one- or two-sentence hook describing your story line. Reducing your idea to one or two lines helps you to focus on your bare-bones plot, keeping you on track as you write. If you have a lot of trouble coming up with your pitch, it could mean your plot is not tight enough or your main character's conflict is not clear or compelling enough. Working with your pitch line can indicate when it's time to go back to the plotting board.

PART
TWO

THE PACKAGE

▲

CHAPTER FIVE

GIVE 'EM WHAT THEY WANT

"I love being a writer. What I can't stand is the paperwork."

—Peter De Vries

You have refined your pitch for conferences, and maybe by now you've had a chance to test it. You've also crafted a compelling query letter and started sending it out. Within days, sometimes weeks, sometimes longer, your familiar SASEs start arriving in your mailbox. It's an exciting time, rushing to tear open the flap to see what's inside.

But in many ways, it's as if you entered a sweepstakes—and we all know what the odds are there. Be prepared for rejection. It's inevitable—the name of the game. You'll find some tips on how to deal with it in chapter eight.

Most solid acceptances come by way of telephone. (That thinly packed SASE most likely will hold a rejection letter.) When your pitch or query earns you a positive response, you'll be asked to send more. They'll tell you what to send, and our motto is Give 'Em What They Want.

If an agent asks for sample chapters, don't give in to your temptation to send in your entire manuscript. And conversely, if someone requests your entire manuscript, don't send in a partial work with an apologetic note saying you haven't finished it yet. You shouldn't be querying unless your manuscript is finished.

THE SUBMISSION PACKAGE

What constitutes an effective submission package? Sample chapters or the complete manuscript make up the backbone. The SASE is understood. Even if it isn't requested, you're expected to send one. (In some cases, you'll need to send two SASEs. We'll explain that further on.) A cover letter might not be requested either, but it should definitely be included. Many agents and editors will ask for a synopsis or a chapter outline, too.

Let's look at each element separately.

SAMPLE CHAPTERS

When a beginning writer received her first request for more—in this case a sample chapter—she dutifully pored through her entire manuscript in search of the best chapters. When she reached chapter twenty-four she felt she'd found a good enough sample. It had all the right elements: suspense, action, snappy dialogue, a cliff-hanger chapter ending. She soon learned that when agents or editors ask for sample chapters, they aren't asking for your *best* chapters; they want to see your *first* chapters.

She also learned that *all* chapters have to be "best" chapters. Chapter twenty-four was good enough to compel a few agents to overlook this writer's mistake, and they requested the complete manuscript from her. And then they turned it down. Chapter twenty-four of that first attempt had promised something the rest of the manuscript couldn't deliver at the time.

A request for sample chapters more often than not means chapters one through three. It doesn't mean chapters three, eight and twenty-four.

Sometimes agents and editors will get more specific and request the first fifty or one hundred pages. But what if chapter three ends on page 53? Should you just send the first fifty pages and leave that chapter incomplete? A couple of extra pages won't upset an agent or editor, and it's fine to send those pages along so the chapter isn't left hanging.

But here's a trick savvy writers all know. When you're writing that novel, keep in mind you're most likely going to have to send the first fifty or one hundred pages or chapters one through three. Design your chapters so they end in the right place. You can always reorganize them later and divide them up differently. But knowing what you'll be asked for can help you prepare in advance how you lay out your book.

What about that pesky prologue you've written for your book? Does that count as part of the first fifty pages? Would a request for the first three chapters mean the prologue, too? If they ask for only the first chapter, should you send the prologue or chapter one?

Here's a rule of thumb to guide you. If the prologue is set in a completely different time or place than the rest of your novel, don't send it. An example is William Peter Blatty's famous book *The Exorcist*. The prologue follows a religious figure through an unspecified desert during an unspecified time period and is diametrically opposed to the setting and tone—contemporary Washington, DC—established in chapter one. Our guess is that when he was asked for more, he left the prologue home and submitted the first three chapters.

If your prologue is an integral part of the story, set in the same time period and in the same location as the rest of your book, then count that as part of the first fifty pages.

Why do agents and editors just ask for samples? Why don't they request the whole thing? Agent Kathleen Anderson says, "When I ask for just sample chapters, it's not because I'm less interested than I might be with someone else's query. It's because the success of the story for me will lie in the writing, and I can usually judge whether or not the writing works for me by just a few chapters."

COMPLETE MANUSCRIPT

Many agents and editors agree with Kathleen Anderson, but not all. Some feel that once they've started reading those first three chapters and are hooked, they don't want to have to wait for the rest of the manuscript. Those agents and editors will always request you send in the complete manuscript—the finished product. "I prefer to see the entire book," says agent George Nicholson. "For me, one or two chapters isn't enough to tell whether the book is salable. Besides, the less busywork I can get involved in, the better. If I receive only a partial, and I'm interested enough to ask for the whole book, requesting the rest of the book means more work on my part. But it's different for every agent."

PRESENTATION, PRESENTATION, PRESENTATION

Although what you write and how you write it is the most important consideration, the presentation of your overall submission package will also make an impression. The trick is to make a good impression.

"I don't like submissions that are sloppily put together," editor John Scognamiglio says. "Whatever you submit should be professionally presented. It should be neatly typed, with margins and a nice cover letter. The presentation is what first catches my eye."

While a package that follows all the standard conventions won't guarantee you representation or publication, one that breaks the rules will probably hurt your chances.

Following the Rules

Some writers are tempted to pull out all stops when submitting their manuscript. They resort to gimmicks and even gifts, and they don't realize that the writing alone is what will get a foot in the door.

"Sometimes I get a fancy package with the manuscript bound together like a book, tied with ribbons and that sort of thing," says John Scognamiglio. "I need loose pages. I carry the manuscripts around with me. Or maybe I need to make a copy of it so somebody else can read it."

"There are the people who send chocolates and other little gifts," says editor Ginjer Buchanan, "which might be cute but won't make the least bit of difference in the evaluation of your manuscript. The one that has gone down as legend, though, is the writer who sent his manuscript in a hand-tooled leather binder inside a hand-carved wooden box! He didn't even send return postage, and he was from Canada. Apparently he thought fancy packaging would get our attention. It got a reaction, but not the one he was hoping for. His ploy couldn't disguise the fact that the manuscript wasn't very good. So don't send us distracting gifts or manuscripts on strange paper or in fancy boxes. If your writing is good, if your ideas are fresh, and if it is appropriate for us, then your work will get noticed."

Agent Evan Marshall says, "I get things on pink paper with perfume sprinkled over them and wrapped with ribbons. I get things printed on both sides of the page."

He gets them and then he rejects them.

So that won't happen to you, follow our step-by-step guidelines.

Manuscript Formatting

1. Use good quality, 8½″ × 11″ (22cm × 28cm) white paper (no onion skin).
2. Type on only one side of the page.
3. Double-space your manuscript. (One-page query letters and synopses should be single-spaced, but anything over one page must be double-spaced.)
4. Indent each paragraph, and do not insert an extra space between paragraphs—you can, however, leave an extra space between scene changes.
5. Use a good laser or ink-jet printer. Dot matrix is out.
6. Place your name, book title and page number on the first line of each page. It should look like this:

   King/Insomnia   3

   (Most word processing packages have a heading function that can do this for you.)
7. Leave ample margins (¾″ to 1″ [1.9cm to 2.5cm]) on all four sides of all pages.
8. Do not justify your manuscript's right margin; leave the edges ragged.

9. Drop down a quarter or half page to start a new chapter.
10. Include a cover page with your manuscript. Put your name, address, phone number and approximate or exact word count on the cover page. See the sidebar for a sample cover page.
11. Type "The End" on the last page.
12. To protect the last page from getting soiled, place a blank piece of paper at the end.

A Word on Copyright

There is no need to display the copyright symbol on your manuscript. You also don't need it on your cover letter, your synopsis, your chapter outline or even on your sample chapters. The copyright laws automatically protect you before your work sees print. Generally, the publisher takes care of filing the copyright notice for you, inserting the copyright formula in your book and registering your book with the Library of Congress. Most standard publishing contracts call for the copyright to be issued in your name.

As an aspiring author, you should know all this. Including the copyright notice on your submission marks you as an amateur. Also, it might send a most unwanted, negative message: "I don't trust you." That's no way to start a conversation, especially not when you're asking someone to risk time, money and reputation on you.

SASEs

With your submission package you must enclose a no. 10 (business size) SASE. You hope the agent or editor will use it to send an acceptance letter. However, most acceptances of this nature come by telephone, so by default, if that SASE is used, it will most likely be to enclose your rejection letter. It might seem like negative thinking to send it along, as if you're inviting rejection, but send it along you must. If your acceptance comes by phone, your SASE will either be dumped, or if the agent or editor hasn't lost it by then, it might be used to send your contract.

If you want your manuscript returned, you must also enclose a

Your Name **❶**   **❷** Word count

Street Address

City, State, Zip Code

Phone number, E-mail address

TITLE

❸

BY

YOUR NAME

1. Your information is placed in the upper left-hand corner.
2. The word count is placed in the upper right-hand corner.
3. The title and your byline are centered halfway down the page.

larger self-addressed, stamped mailer. But in these days of laser printers and relatively low photocopying charges, many writers prefer not
to pay the extra postage. They include a small note at the end of
their cover letter, sometimes in a postscript, that the manuscript is
recyclable and need not be returned.

Having the manuscript returned may be an unneccessary expendi-
ture of money and effort. Agents and editors want to feel as if they are
the first to read your manuscript. To help foster that feeling, it's a
good idea to send only a fresh manuscript. As careful as agents and
editors try to be, it's inevitable that a coffee ring or a splotch of jelly
from their lunchtime PB&J sandwich will end up on one or more of
your pages. Why waste the return postage if you're just going to have
to recycle the manuscript yourself?

Most agents and editors are accustomed to this practice and think
nothing of tossing the manuscript into the recycle bin. Agent Evan
Marshall, though, has a different slant—one you can take into consideration when making your decision on how to approach this issue. "I
think people should care that their work be returned to them. They
should think that this is their baby, even if it comes back dog-eared
and unusable. Whenever I send something to an editor I ask for it
back. No agent tells an editor to throw it away. You're sending a
subliminal message that this is valuable. It wouldn't make me not take
someone on, but everything I have taken on has come with an envelope to send it back."

COVER LETTER

Although you might not be asked specifically to send a cover letter
with your manuscript submission, not sending one is like making a
phone call and refusing to speak when your party picks up.

The purpose of the cover letter is to reintroduce yourself briefly
(you made your initial introduction through your query letter or at
that writers conference) and identify what you are submitting. You
can't assume that the recipient of your submission knows what's inside

or will want to figure it out by going through the material. For more help with cover letters, turn to chapter seven.

SYNOPSIS

Simply put, a synopsis is a summary of your book's story. Agents and editors often request a synopsis with your submission package. Some will read it first before settling down with your manuscript; some even use it to decide if they will read your manuscript at all. Others save the synopsis until they've read your manuscript. Writing a synopsis is a task even successful writers dread. The good news is that the more successful you get, the less often you have to write a synopsis. Even better news is that in chapter six you'll see that writing the synopsis doesn't have to be as painful as you might think.

CHAPTER OUTLINE

Although the term *outline* is often used synonymously with *synopsis*, these are separate entities. Some agents or editors request an outline, which expands the synopsis and gives a running summary of your novel, chapter by chapter. You'll learn more about the chapter outline in chapter six.

Turning Sawdust Into Gold

Long before Elmore Leonard became one of North America's most popular and prolific novelists, he wrote a treatment for a western yarn he called *Legends* and tried to sell it to the movies. "I would write a book on spec," he says, "but not a screenplay." He had been immersing himself in western lore and was able to write the treatment without much new research.

The treatment failed to sell as a film, but Marc Jaffe, an editor at Bantam Books, asked Leonard to do a western novel, and Leonard used the *Legends* treatment to write the book. "Emmett Long" from the treatment became "Dana Moon" in the book. "If I wrote any more westerns," Leonard explains, "I planned to use Emmett Long as a pseudonym"—something he never did.

Legends is the essence of a compelling synopsis—a good plot in an authentic setting, rendered crisply and with a good dose of Leonard's famous dialogue for flavor. It's long, but it reads short. And it shows how you can turn the sawdust of a failed project into gold. The *Legends* synopsis is reproduced here (pp. 107-114).

(Note: Although Leonard uses past tense here, we recommend that you use present tense for your synopses.)

AGENT AND EDITOR ETIQUETTE (YOURS, NOT THEIRS)

Once you've sent in the requested "more," the wait begins. We admit that this can be difficult to deal with for some people, and in chapter eight you'll find tips to help you through it. But now's a good time to look at a few more important rules that might be tempting to break at this stage of the process.

Believe it or not, some new writers, with absolutely no track record and absolutely no reason to think they could get away with it, are demanding, overbearing, aggressive—and just plain rude. They make unpleasant phone calls; they write unpleasant letters. The quality of your work is not the only element evaluated by an agent or editor considering a business relationship with you. Successful relationships are long term; no one wants to work with someone who is arrogant.

While brewing new plots and honing your craft takes time and effort, providing a turnoff is quick and easy.

But avoiding one is just as easy. Here are some examples of blatant turnoffs; steer clear of them.

Turnoff #1: Inappropriate Phone Calls

There are times you can call to check on your manuscript. If it was solicited material and you haven't heard within the response time reported in the market guide listing, adding another week of waiting time, then making a polite call during business hours is appropriate. The situations on pp. 115-116 are not.

LEGENDS
By Elmore Leonard

Two riders came down out of the Sierra Madres and recrossed the Rio Grande with their prisoner: a one-eyed renegade Nimbre Apache named Lobo, who had jumped the reservation at San Carlos and was said to have taken part in the White Tanks massacre. They brought in Lobo and a young white woman, Carla Wells, the Apache had been dragging along with him since White Tanks. (They said they had to keep the young woman away from Lobo or she would have caved his head in with a rock.) They set the young woman free, returning her to what was left of her family, and delivered Lobo to the military lockup at Fort Huachuca.

For their trouble, both men were kicked out of the Army.

Emmett Long—a stringy cowboy turned contract guide, who was accepted as a brother by his Apache trackers and could read sign right along with them—was fired on the spot.

Brendan Early—after ten years on frontier station, 2nd Lt. of Cavalry ("the Dandy 5th") and after telling the Department of Arizona what he thought of their candy-ass procedures—was forced to resign his commission.

They had gotten their man, but "without written authority to cross the border into Mexico to undertake an extended campaign . . . and without the necessary complement of troops."

So there they were: loose, easygoing Emmett Long and Brendan Early, the long-haired swashbuckler, sitting in a saloon in Contention, Arizona, looking out at the desert. Em got talking to a man who was district superintendent for Hatch & Hodges, the stage line company, and found out they were expanding their service and needed a steady supply of fresh horses. So Em rounded up some of his White Mountain trackers and went into the horse business as a mustanger, halterbreaking green mounts and delivering them to the company's line stations.

continued on next page

Bren Early tried organizing and guiding for hunting parties—taking rich Easterners out for a look at the Wild West
and a chance to shoot big horn and mule deer. The trouble was, Bren's
temperament got in the way. He could stand hip-cocked and show
them how to fan a six-shooter and keep a bean can jumping. But he
didn't have the patience to wait on tourists, no matter how much they
paid him. So Bren quit the hunting guide business and went into
holding up Hatch & Hodges stagecoaches, the same company that
was supporting Emmett.

Bren was caught at it and sentenced to ten years of hard labor at a
work camp out in the desert, where convicts lived in cages and busted
rocks building a road to nowhere.

Em, in the meantime, had gotten something going with Carla
Wells—the young lady they'd rescued—and finally married her. She
was a cute little thing, but salty talking and with a hard bark on her.
Yes, she'd marry Emmett, but she wasn't going to live in any horse
camp. She had him buy her a boarding house in Contention. That was
where he could find her when he wasn't out in the bleak lonesome
busting his ass.

Emmett was out there with his White Mountain boys one day when
he happened across his old buddy Brendan Early chopping rocks on
the road gang.

Bren said, "Sweet saving Jesus, get me out of here, will you?"

Em thought it was pretty funny. The head guard, a son of a bitch
named Brazil, didn't think it was funny at all and got mean with
Emmett and ran him off with shotguns, scattering Em's herd. The
head guard shouldn't have done that.

Emmett plotted and figured out a way to spring Bren loose without
anyone getting seriously hurt. Bren promised to lead a pure life and
not get in any trouble again. He went off prospecting for gold.

Emmett, about this time, was contacted by an official in the Department of the Interior and offered the job of Indian Agent at the

continued on next page

Stone River Reservation. The money wasn't much, but Em was offered good land, too, the opportunity to develop his own spread, and Carla said it was OK with her. So Em got into the business of supervising life on an Indian reservation—handling serious human rights situations as well as petty squabbles—while operating a horse ranch on the side, keeping on his White Mountain Apaches, a good bunch to have in a tight spot.

Bren Early the gold prospector staked out claims in the mountains and hit pay dirt a couple of times. His trouble was not only impatience but holding onto his money. Bren was a big spender, and so eager to find gold he didn't realize right away he was sitting on a bonanza lode of copper. When this was discovered, the big-big company Dorado Mining moved in, gave Bren the full treatment with booze and broads and visions of vast wealth. As a result, Dorado was able to buy a controlling interest in Bren's holdings and set him up as a company vice-president in charge of local operations.

Emmett Long had been dealing with a minor problem ever since he became an Indian Agent. Some of his charges had left the reservation to live up in the nearby mountains, where they were able to irrigate and develop rich plots of farmland—holdings that were small but adequate to their needs. Along with the reservation Indians in the mountains, there was a scattering of Chicano homesteads and even a small community of Black people.

The spokesman for the Chicanos was a revolutionary type named Santana who was always bitching about something—the encroachment of the Indians—or looking for the Big Cause, some way he could be martyred.

The elder of the Black community was an ex-Tenth Cavalry sergeant named Billy Goss, who was an old friend of Emmett's. The two of them liked to track up into high country for a few days at a time, hunt mule deer and drink whiskey and get away from their women.

Everything was going fine until the Bureau of Indian Affairs in-

continued on next page

formed Emmett he had to get his people down out of the mountains and back to the reservation.

What for? Nobody owned the land or was using it. But that's where he was wrong. Dorado Mining had taken out leases on large tracts and they were going in there to dynamite and test for copper lodes.

Shit, well let them test and if they didn't find any copper then let them get their equipment out of there. No, the Bureau said, the Indians had to get back on the reservation anyway.

But what about all the other people living up there? Well, if they didn't clear out it was tough shit if somebody got hurt.

You know who the first one was to get it. Emilio Santana. He wouldn't budge, took a bullet in the chest and died smiling.

Then the Black community was hit in a brutal raid that left several innocent people dead, including Billy Goss.

Emmett wired the Bureau, but they'd washed their hands of the situation. It was a local matter now, under the jurisdiction of the District Court. Emmett went to court, but what kind of suit could he file? His people were trespassing and the legal owners had a right to protect their property.

By this time, skirmishes were going on in the hills, both sides sniping at each other, people getting killed. It became known in the press as the Dragoon Mountains War.

Next, Emmett rode to the Dorado Mining Company offices in Contention and asked to see the man in charge. When they told him to leave and tried to throw him out, he kicked the door down and stood there face-to-face with Brendan Early. So they drank whiskey and discussed the situation, and Emmett didn't like the tone of it at all. Bren's attitude was: Why should Emmett worry? Those people didn't mean anything to him. Emmett said they had years staked in their land and the dynamiting was messing up their watersheds and running off their livestock. The chances were the company wouldn't find any ore; they'd pull out and leave the poor people ruined. It wasn't fair.

continued on next page

So when was life fair? Bren said. It was too bad, but that's the way it was.

On the way home, Emmett was stopped by a couple of company gunmen. They tried to have a little fun with him, scare him. When Emmett didn't flinch or back down, they got uglier and Emmett was forced to pull his gun and kill one of them. The next day he was arrested, charged with murder and placed in the Contention jail.

It bothered Bren that he couldn't help Emmett and call off his dogs. But now his allegiance was to the company, and money. When Emmett was arrested, though, it gave Bren the opportunity to return a favor and even their account. He told Emmett he could bribe a deputy and spring him loose if he wanted. Emmett said fine, but if he was allowed to walk out, he was going to ride up into the hills and finish this business, one way or another.

Emmett returned home to find his house burned down, his herd scattered and Carla hiding in the woods. If he had any misgivings before, they were gone now. He got his wife, rounded up his White Mountain boys and rode up into high country.

Bren Early found he didn't have the clout he thought he did. When he tried to get the company to ease up, he was told his office had nothing to do with public relations. The man in charge of that job was a known gunman by the name of Sundeen, who had little or no respect for Bren Early, vice-president or not. So there was Bren with his house, his money, his ladies; but feeling pretty rotten and not able to rationalize his way out of it. What the hell was he supposed to do?

Emmett knew what to do. It wasn't even a matter of choice now. The fact that in the long run he couldn't win and probably would be shot dead was not a consideration. He'd stand with his people and the big company was going to suffer great pain and expense before this was through.

He said to Carla, "What do you think?" And she said to him, "When you're right, honey, stand up and kick ass." She was a sweet

continued on next page

girl and would be there with him, because there was no sending her away.

The Company posted a $5,000 reward for Emmett Long, dead or alive. Bren Early resented it. How come Emmett was getting all the attention?

Newspaper people came out to Contention and roamed the countryside trying to get a glimpse of the Dragoon Mountains War. They took pictures of reservation Apaches, peaceful Navahos and Lipans, holding old Army Springfields and muzzle-loaders. They posed Sundeen and his bunch in front of the Gold Dollar, getting them to display every weapon they owned and borrowed a few more, sticking the revolvers in their belts.

Sundeen ate it up . . .

Until Emmett, with a big-bore .50 caliber Sharps, blew Sundeen out of his saddle at 480 measured yards, shattering the man's right arm and breaking some ribs. Sundeen went home, wherever that was.

Still, there were plenty of shooters to be hired at $25 a week who would take their rifles and some chuck and go up into the high country. Some of them did not come back. Those who did shook their heads and said there wasn't anybody up there—as though Emmett Long and his White Mountain boys were sitting on stumps waiting to be seen.

The mining company dynamite crews didn't see them either, though they'd wake up to find all their powder and stores had disappeared in the night. How could you fight a man who didn't show himself? Armed men would sneak up on a rancheria and there wouldn't be a soul there or anything worth burning. They'd get back down to the draw where they'd left their horses and find them gone.

Meanwhile Emmett and his ghost band had hit another mine camp and put the fear of hell in men waking up bug-eyed in the night.

When the newspapers began laughing at the big important company, somebody at the company said, "Enough, get it done." So they mustered a couple hundred hard cases and hoboes in Contention, fed

continued on next page

and armed them and sent them up to kill that worrisome son of a bitch once and for all. Kill him or don't come back.

Bren Early said good-bye to the good life and rode out an hour ahead of them—rode out of Contention as he had ridden out of Cairo, Illinois, twenty-two years ago, to join in the Indian Wars before they were over. What in hell had he been sitting on the fence for when Emmett was getting all the glory? What was important in life anyway?

Bren placed $500 in bets at the Gold Dollar that Emmett Long would never be shot dead nor taken alive . . . left an envelope in the local newspaper office marked "PRINT AT ONCE" . . . and lashed a case of good bourbon to his pack animal in case Emmett had run out of corn.

The message the newspaper typesetter took out of the envelope and put on his machine said: $10,000 REWARD—DEAD OR ALIVE, and the name under it, specified in even bigger letters, BRENDAN EARLY.

Emmett welcomed Bren with a feeling of apprehension. He trusted him, but . . . what was going on? What was Bren so tickled about if he'd come over to join the doomed? Emmett wondered if Bren had put himself in this fight-to-the-death situation for the sole purpose of regaining his self-respect. Was that how Bren looked at it? It gave Emmett a strange feeling. Like they were putting this show on just for Bren.

Emmett knew the mining company army was on its way. He'd already sent his scouts out to act as decoys, to lure the ragtag army into a box canyon. Emmett believed the plan had a slim chance of working and could save their lives if it did. But to lure them in so easily—he couldn't believe it when the two hundred armed men, under some fool who thought he was a general, marched eagerly into the canyon and stood there under Emmett's gun like they were anxious to be killed.

"A gesture," Brendan said. "The company wants out, but they can't do it with egg on their face, so they send these rummies and drifters, thinking to smother you with numbers."

continued on next page

Emmett had settled his mind about dying, if it was to come. But he wasn't going to shed blood for a company press release—for the newspaper people and photographers climbing up to his position, wanting to get pictures, they said, of both sides of the action.

Or for the man in tailored buckskins and white whiskers who came up to Emmett and said, "Sign here. If you get through this, Mr. Long, I want you in our Real and Authentic Rip-Roaring Wild West Show."

Emmett's White Mountain Apaches and the tough Chicano farmers and the hard-eyed survivors from the Black settlement, they all looked at him. What was going on? Brendan Early drew matched revolvers and said, "Come on. Let's get to it."

Not yet aware.

Now Carla was looking at him. She said, "What are we doing here?"

Emmett said, "I don't know. I didn't see it happening, but it's over."

The White Mountain boys had already felt it and were disappearing, moving off one by one. The Chicanos and the Blacks stood looking at Emmett a little longer. Now they began to walk away.

Emmett turned to Brendan Early. He said, "You're too late for your glory." He looked around to see all his people gone. "And I've stayed too long."

It stopped Brendan. What, never again face death and feel the kick of his six-shooters? It took Bren a minute or so to readjust; not much longer than that.

He looked at the man in the tailored buckskins and white whiskers, thought a moment, then looked at Emmett. "We're paid up," Bren said, "rode hard and lived to tell about it. That's worth more than something. You want to stoop in a cornfield or walk tall down the main drag?"

The man in the tailored buckskins was waiting.

Emmett thought hard and said to Carla, "It wouldn't hurt to see the sights, would it?" Carla said to him, "You're the sights. You and your partner." But she'd go along. What the hell.

Emmett looked over at Brendan. He said, "Let's see what's next."

THE MIDDLE-OF-THE-NIGHT PHONE CALL

Kent Brown, founder of Boyds Mills Press, reveals the worst experience he ever had with a writer:

> 3:25 A.M., my phone rings. The voice on the other end says, "Kent Brown?"
>
> I said, "Yes."
>
> "Kent L. Brown?"
>
> "Yes."
>
> "You work at Highlights for Children?"
>
> "Yes."
>
> Now, I have three children. And this sounds to me just the way the state police would contact you when they have a cadaver that belongs to you. I was beginning to get very stressed.
>
> Then the caller said, "I need to get published."
>
> I said, "You can't call me in the middle of the night," and hung up.
>
> And she called back.
>
> I went into the other room and said, "OK, tell me what your name is."
>
> She did, then said, "You won't hold this against me?"
>
> I said, "I certainly will," and hung up. I believe that is the only time in twenty-eight years I ever hung up on an author.

THE "BUT WHY? BUT WHY?" PHONE CALL

Bantam Books editor Wendy McCurdy says turnoffs for her are calls from writers asking why their work was rejected. "That always puts me in an awkward position, because I will never say to a person that I rejected something because it was terrible. So what does that leave me to say if that was the case? All I can say is I get so many submissions, I just don't remember. I don't want to be responsible for affecting a person's life that way."

"Arguing with my decision doesn't help," editor Michael Seidman says. "In fact, it's only going to work against you with future submissions. Editors are only human (although some are willing to accept deification). If I had a sleepless night, I'm not going to be in a good mood. So stay cool and professional, show the respect that anyone deserves (as we try to show you that respect by reading what you send) and keep your fingers crossed."

THE "DID IT GET THERE YET?" PHONE CALL

Agent Nancy Love says, "I dislike writers who call and ask if I received their manuscript. This can easily be remedied by sending a self-addressed stamped postcard along with the manuscript."

Editor Nancy Bereano says, "Don't call to follow up on a manuscript. If a publisher has a reputation for not losing manuscripts and for responding, and the publisher says she will get back in two to four weeks, then just assume the publisher will do that. I won't talk to people on the phone about why we rejected their manuscript or how soon we'll get back to them."

Turnoff #2: Gimmicks

Evan Marshall says, "I get a lot of books with the hero named Evan. This has happened too often for me to think it's coincidence. In these days of 'find and replace', I picture all these writers sitting at their computers, changing the main characters' names depending upon the agent to whom they are submitting. Just imagine a historical novel with an Evan and a Binky."

And, if you're writing science fiction, for example, don't think you'll impress an editor or agent by claiming you've visited other planets. Although you might get a laugh, it probably won't result in an acceptance.

Turnoff #3: Hard-on-the-Eyes Manuscripts

"I prefer to be sent clean copy," agent Nancy Yost says. "It doesn't have to be on a laser printer, but handwritten ones are out. And I hate to admit it, but there's always a bit of a psychological prejudice against manuscripts produced on an old typewriter. All that Wite-Out. You want to feel your writers are current, using computers."

Agent Evan Marshall says, "The old nine-pin dot matrix printer is a horrible turnoff. If you can't afford a laser printer, then consider bringing the disk to a print shop and having them print it out. An ink-jet printer is fine or even a twenty-four-pin dot matrix printer with letter quality."

Turnoff #4: Improper Manuscript Formatting

"Be sure that the manuscript is double-spaced and that the pages are numbered," agent Susan Zeckendorf says. "These are things that people don't necessarily do."

Agent Pesha Rubinstein says, "Manuscripts *must* be double-spaced. You wouldn't believe how many projects get submitted to me that are still single-spaced. It's hard on the eyes; you can't read it. The same with dot matrix printers. Without our eyes we can't do anything in this business."

Agent Evan Marshall says, "I get manuscripts with no indentations for paragraphs, but extra space between the paragraphs."

Proper formatting means double-spaced copy; ¾" to 1" (1.9cm to 2.5cm) margins on top, sides and bottom; and each paragraph indented with no extra space between paragraphs.

Turnoff #5: Overdone Manuscript Packaging

"In any industry there are rules you usually follow, and not to shows you're an amateur, not aware of the conventions," says agent Evan Marshall. "I get things packed so tight that it's like a Brink's truck. My secretary and I hack away at it with sledgehammers and axes to get it open, and by the time it's open we barely want to look at it. All you really need to do is put your manuscript in a box and then put it in a simple mailer and staple it four times. You don't need rubber bands, bubble wrap, duct tape, newspaper or Jiffy Bags with stuffing so we have to vacuum every day."

Turnoff #6: Queries and Submissions via Faxes and E-mail

"Faxes are a turnoff," says agent Evan Marshall. "I'm old-fashioned. For me the fax suggests urgency or convenience for people you're already dealing with. And most of us still use the thermal paper and, psychologically, that's never going to look as good as a nice crisp letter. And of course an SASE can't accompany a fax."

Editor Kent Brown says, "We don't want manuscripts by E-mail, and we don't want disks. Over time, I don't know what we are going to do about E-mail, but I worry about it because it's so easy to reject something on a computer screen.

"Most of the manuscripts get read in somebody's bed or armchair. So far, it's easier to read black type on paper than it is on a computer screen."

▲▼

The way you prepare and submit your manuscript can make a good impression—or turn an agent off. While not all transgressions are major, and many do border on overly picky, they can add up to convey an unfavorable image. There's certainly humor in some of them, but unless you're a comedy writer, you don't want an agent or editor laughing at your unconventional approach. The idea is to be taken seriously.

Getting published is hard enough; don't make it more difficult for yourself. Learning the conventions and following through with them might even impress the person you were thoughtful enough not to annoy.

SIMULTANEOUS SUBMISSIONS

In chapter three we pointed out the dos and don'ts for submitting query letters simultaneously. Submitting manuscripts simultaneously is a different story, though, especially if an agent has asked for an exclusive read. Many do nowadays, because of the pressure of competition. Although it takes little time to respond to a query, a lot more

Submission Dos and Don'ts

1. ***Don't*** bind your manuscript. You can place one large elastic band around it to hold the pages loosely together.
2. ***Don't*** use staples on any submissions.
3. ***Don't*** overwrap your manuscript.
4. ***Don't*** send it registered or insured. Requiring agents or editors to sign for packages is an inconvenience for them.
5. ***Don't*** send your only copy.
6. ***Do*** remember to enclose your SASEs—a no. 10 for the reply, a large mailer for the return of the manuscript, and a SASP so the agent or editor can notify you they received the manuscript.
7. ***Do*** your homework before sending anything out. Know who you are submitting your work to. Request guidelines, sample copies and/or catalogs.
8. ***Don't*** call in a few days to ask the agent if he or she received your manuscript.
9. ***Do*** learn the jargon. For example, know the difference between a multiple submission and a simultaneous submission (see chapter three for an explanation). ***Don't*** make such costly mistakes as calling your work a fictional novel. (All novels are fiction—the redundancy shows amateur status.)
10. ***Do*** send your work to reputable publishing houses and literary agencies. Know the scams and what to avoid. *Don't* pay reading fees or jump to bite at a contract that comes asking you for money.
11. ***Do*** show from your correspondence or phone conversations that you are an agreeable, flexible person. Agents take personality into account when deciding whom to represent. Editors can be put off from accepting a book if the writer is impossible to deal with.

effort goes into reading an entire manuscript, and it's understandable if an exclusive read is a requirement.

Here's how you can deal with it. Most agents include their need for an exclusive read in their market guide listings. If you don't want to lose the time that would involve, don't query that agent.

Even if this requirement isn't listed, they'll tell you about it if and when they respond positively to your query. Now you have to decide if this is an agent you'd really like to work with. (If he or she isn't, you really shouldn't have bothered querying in the first place.) If so, then it's worth your while to grant the exclusive. One thing you can do, though, is (politely) provide a four- to six-week time limit for the exclusive. If the agent goes over that time limit and you have others waiting, a (polite) follow-up note or even a phone call is allowed.

What if your manuscript is already out elsewhere on an exclusive read when the request for another exclusive comes in? It's all a matter of timing. You can wait to hear back from the first agent before you send the manuscript out again. No one is waiting impatiently for your manuscript to arrive. They've put the request in the mail to you and have gone on to other things. There's no need for you to write the second agent and tell her it will be a couple of weeks before you can send the material to her. In New York a couple of weeks goes by like, well, a New York minute.

New writers often ask us, "But what if after I send my manuscript out to four or five agents, four or five want to represent me? Or what if more than one publishing house wants to accept my book?"

Of course, it can happen. But more often it doesn't. OK, it almost *never* happens. But—and that's a big *but*—if it should, then go with the agent you feel will represent you best and write polite letters declining the others' services.

If more than one *publisher* is vying for your book, get on the phone and call the agent you want to represent you—and pass him the baton. The agent will work out the best deal for you.

Final Checklist

When those requests for more start coming in, be ready for them. Here's a checklist to help keep yourself organized.

1. Photocopy several sets of your first three chapters as well as your complete manuscript.

2. Have your one-page synopsis ready to go.

3. Make sure the cover letter you've prepared to accompany your submission packet is personally addressed to the agent or editor: reminds her that your material is solicited; and states your genre, word count and a one- or two-line description of the plot.

4. Prepare enough no. 10 SASEs to include in your submissions. Mention in your cover letter that it is not necessary to return the manuscript or enclose a large postage-paid mailer for the manuscript's return.

5. Keep a list of all agents and editors you have queried, the dates you heard from them and sent the requested material, and an itemization of what each submission packet contains.

CHAPTER
SIX

SUCCESSFUL SYNOPSES

"My agent says she can tell how good a novel will be on the basis of a short synopsis. My editor says she can, too. But I can't, and I'm the one who has to write the blasted novel."

—Robyn Carr (*Mind Tryst, Tempted, Informed Risk*)

I f all goes well with the querying or pitching process, the agent or editor will ask to see more. In addition to sample chapters or your complete manuscript, more almost always includes a synopsis.

So, what is a synopsis? It's a summary with feeling. It's a good read with strong narrative writing in the present tense. And it's an important tool for getting an agent or publisher for your novel.

It is not a blow-by-blow, scene-by-scene outline. Some agents or editors may use the terms *outline* and *synopsis* interchangeably, but don't be confused. Unless the agent specifically asks for a chapter-by-chapter outline, you'll use the synopsis for your initial submission.

While a chapter outline may run to dozens of pages (see the example on pp. 183-185), your synopsis must be short. You'll need to summarize your story in just a few pages. Many agents and editors require a synopsis of no longer than a single page!

Don't panic. You can give them exactly what they want. You're learning to create pitch lines and queries. A synopsis draws on those same approaches and skills you're already developing.

If you still find the prospect of writing a synopsis daunting, you're not alone.

"Everyone I know hates to write a synopsis," says science fiction novelist Kiel Stuart. "I hate doing them a little less because I wrote film treatments, and novel synopses are similar to those. Both are told in present tense and summarize the action to one degree or other."

"I had to write a half a dozen novels before I could sell based on a synopsis," best-selling novelist Dean Koontz says. "I hated writing a synopsis. Beginning with *Strangers*, I stopped writing outlines altogether."

He's one of the lucky ones. Koontz and other mega-selling authors don't have to write a synopsis for each novel anymore. "I send 'em the book; they publish it," Stephen King says. "It's a great deal. And give me credit for this: I'm smart enough to be grateful."

Until you reach the level of a Dean Koontz or a Stephen King, the synopsis is an essential tool for selling your novel.

WHY WRITING A SYNOPSIS IS SO DIFFICULT

Here are three very good reasons why a synopsis is difficult to write:

I. A SYNOPSIS IS DIFFERENT FROM A NOVEL. As a novelist, you tell stories—long stories. You use narration to create compelling representations of reality. You've learned to show, not tell. Now you're faced with the prospect of having to summarize your story.

If you'd wanted to write summaries, you'd have gotten a job with Cliffs Notes writing study guides, right?

2. A SYNOPSIS SHOULD READ LIKE A NOVEL. If in summarizing your story in a few brilliantly chosen paragraphs, you reduce it to bloodless "synopsis speak," if it reads like a series of "and then he . . . and then she . . . and then they . . . ," you won't like writing it and, more importantly, an agent or editor won't like reading it.

If they don't like reading it, they simply stop.

Why Dick Francis Has Never Had to Write a Synopsis

I'm afraid you will probably find my answer to your query . . . somewhat disappointing," novelist Dick Francis told us when we asked him to share his insights on how to write a winning synopsis. "You see, I have never submitted one!"

But he did tell us how he managed to publish a series of best-sellers without using a selling tool we've been telling you is crucial. Here's his story, in his own words:

"The first book I had published—in 1957—was my autobiography, *The Sport of Queens*, based mostly, up to that time, on my life as a young rider of ponies and horses and, ultimately, as a successful steeplechase jockey. I was persuaded to try my hand at this by an authors agent, Englishman John Johnson. Our mothers were friends, and on one occasion, when John had driven his mother to have tea at my mother's London apartment, he happened to be walking around the apartment looking at photographs on the walls while the two old ladies were conversing about something of no importance. Suddenly, John came across a photograph of the Queen Mother's horse, Devon Loch, collapsing with me in the 1956 Grand National when many lengths in front of any of our rivals, and with only about twenty-five to thirty yards of the race still left to run. It was one of the greatest disasters, not only in racing, but in the whole sporting calendar.

"John immediately got my address and telephone number from my mother and suggested to me that the 'Devon Loch disaster' was an ideal peg on which to 'hang' an autobiography, and why didn't I try my hand at it? After much persuasion from John—and my wife, Mary—I first put pen to paper during the summer of 1956 and finally handed the completed manuscript (which I got permission from Her Majesty to call *The Sport of Queens*) to John during the spring of the following year.

"John said he would take it around the London publishing houses and see if any of them were interested enough to publish, and after I had suggested to him that I had been lucky enough to ride—and win!—on some racehorses owned by publisher Michael Joseph, he immediately took the manuscript to the Joseph publishing house.

"This was followed by Joseph saying that if I wrote one, or perhaps two, more chapters he would be only too pleased to publish. This he did in December 1957, and I'm glad to say it was an immediate success. I had, by this time, retired from being a jockey, this career being immediately followed by that of racing correspondent for the *Sunday Express*, a successful London newspaper.

"One of the conditions of *The Sport of Queens* contract with Michael Joseph Ltd. was that if I ever wrote anything else, Joseph must have priority in seeing the manuscript before any other publisher. So, in late 1961, John Johnson submitted to them the manuscript of my first novel, *Dead Cert*, and this they accepted, and published in the spring of the following year. My second (*Nerve*) and third (*For Kicks*) novels were published in the springs of 1964 and 1965, but on submitting the *For Kicks* manuscript, Joseph said that in order to get me into their 1965 'Christmas Sales' list, they would very much like to have a second manuscript for publication that year. I duly went to work very hard, and the submission of the *Odds Against* manuscript was achieved in time to meet this said list.

"Since then, there has been a new fall Dick Francis novel published in London by Michael Joseph Ltd. and in New York by G.P. Putnam's Sons every year without interruption. I have also done (1986) the biography of the highly successful British jockey Lester Piggott. In London it was titled *Lester* and in New York, *A Jockey's Life*."

So, if you want to be a famous novelist, first become a successful jockey?

> That's not the lesson here. Nor is the notion that if you wait long enough, you'll be discovered. But if you write with the skill and insight of Dick Francis, your novel has a chance of finding a publisher and an audience. If it can happen for a man who rode horses for a living, it can happen for you. ▲

3. A SYNOPSIS LEAVES OUT A LOT OF THE STORY. You'll probably try to tell too much.

You created the story. To you every scene is important (or you wouldn't have included it). But now you must select only the plot high points for your synopsis, perhaps leaving out entire subplots.

It's a tough job—but not nearly as tough as writing a novel! Apply your creativity, your determination and your craft to this new format, and you'll come up with an effective sales tool to help your novel find its audience.

Read on. Once you understand the purpose for your synopsis and the elements it should include, you'll be able to do a fine job.

WHEN TO WRITE THE SYNOPSIS

When is the best time to write the synopsis—before or after you write the book?

Either will work.

If you write your synopsis before you begin the novel, the process will help you create and smooth your plot, and the synopsis can guide you while you write.

The book will probably take on a life of its own as you write it, and you may depart from your synopsis. When that happens, you'll need to go back and rewrite the synopsis.

Once you have an agent for one book, writing the synopsis first for the next book makes a lot of sense. When discussing future projects, you can present your ideas in the one-page synopsis format to get your agent's feedback. If there are any problems with your novel, your agent can make suggestions.

Many writers plan on (or put off) writing the synopsis after the manuscript is finished. Just as with writing the novel, the process of creating a synopsis varies with each writer. You'll need to find your own best way.

Peggy Hoffmann (*Love Potion #9*, *Lady of the Night*) does a great deal of plotting before creating the synopsis. "Before I begin writing, I develop the characters, story goals and setting," she says. "Often, I choose the hero's and heroine's story goals so that they are in conflict with each other. After that, I work out motivation and external conflicts. Then I work on the internal conflict—what keeps the characters from falling in love. Once I have these well in hand, I begin my synopsis."

"A synopsis is one of the last things I do when writing a book," Kiel Stuart says. "Usually I don't think the sort of scribble I do when beginning a novel from scratch (clustering, character and plot sketches) counts as a synopsis."

"What works for me is sitting down and writing the first four or five chapters of a novel, roughly sixty to seventy pages," James A. Ritchie reports. After tinkering and rewriting those first few chapters, "tying up the loose ends, eliminating the wrong turns and so on," Ritchie creates about thirty pages of outline detailing the rest of the novel.

FORMATTING YOUR SYNOPSIS

Keep it simple. Forget cover pages and binders, illustrations and borders, novelty fonts and colored ink. Your characters and conflicts, plus your strong narrative writing, will sell your project.

In the upper left-hand corner, provide
- title
- genre
- word count (approximate)
- your name

Just as with your query and cover letters, you should single-space your one-page synopsis. If the synopsis runs longer than one page single-spaced, then double-space the synopsis. Indent paragraphs, but don't leave extra lines between paragraphs.

Select a readable typeface. Don't go smaller than ten-point type, trying to squeeze more words on a page. Use black ink on white paper. Legibility is the key to the physical presentation.

ELEMENTS OF A SUCCESSFUL SYNOPSIS

"The goal is not to explain the entire book," says novelist James Scott Bell (*The Darwin Conspiracy, Circumstantial Evidence*). "The goal is to get the editor, agent or reader hooked enough to read the sample chapters and to see the market potential."

You need to convey a clear idea of what your book is about, what characters we'll care about (including the ones we'll hate), what's at stake for the main character(s), and how the conflict comes out.

"Basically, we're reading for a sense of characters, conflict—internal and external—and some indication of the setting," says editor Karen Taylor Richman.

Understanding these key elements "can help potential authors write brief but effective synopses instead of dry summarizations of the plot," Bell says.

Your synopsis should usually include

- an opening hook
- quick sketches of the main characters
- plot high points
- the core conflict
- the conclusion

Let's look at each section.

1. The Hook

James A. Ritchie (*The Last Free Range*) reminds us of just how important a good beginning is. "It's the first chapter that matters most," he says. "And perhaps the first page of the first chapter matters most of all. I have a hunch many editors stop reading if the first page or two doesn't hold their interest. So I work on this above all else. Get the opening sentence perfect, make it ask a question the editor/reader wants answered, and you're well on the way to selling a novel."

And as with the novel, so with the novel synopsis. You must start strong. Agents and editors want to be engaged when they're up late at night, plowing through submissions. If they don't like the opening, they won't get through the rest of it.

"Open with a hook, just as you would in a novel," says Marilyn Campbell (*Pretty Maids in a Row, See How They Run*). Your opening few sentences should pull the editor or agent into the synopsis just as your first scene must pull the reader into the novel.

The hook you create for your synopsis probably won't be the opening scene in your novel, but it has to be every bit as involving and engaging as that opening scene. You might use the same opening hook that you provided in your query letter.

Barbara Parker (*Suspicion of Guilt, Suspicion of Innocence, Criminal Justice*) gives her editor a double hook—"a super short spoonful you can gulp down in ten seconds" and then "an expanded version to nibble on."

Here's her "super short spoonful" for the novel *Blood Relations*, published by Dutton.

> The woman whom attorney Thomas Gage loved, then abandoned over twenty years ago, begs him to defend her daughter, a young fashion model charged with murdering the owner of a South Beach night club. Then another murder occurs, and Tom has to confront his past and the recent suicide of his only son to discover the truth.

We've got two murders, family conflict and back story all in two crisp sentences, fifty-seven words.

John Tigges (*The Curse, Evil Dreams*) doesn't waste any time getting to the action with his hook for the synopsis of *Monster*.

Mal and Jonna Evans, in an effort to save their marriage, which has been jeopardized by Jonna's extramarital affair, go backpacking near Garibaldi Provincial Park, British Columbia. On their first night, while preparing their evening meal, a Sasquatch barges into their camp and grabs Jonna.

And we're off.

In the first two sentences, we've got exotic setting (Garibaldi Provincial Park, British Columbia), conflict (a marriage at risk), back story (Jonna's extramarital affair), and, oh yes, the monster.

Robert W. Walker (*Fatal Instinct*, *Razor's Edge*) uses this grabber for *Darkest Instinct*.

FBI Medical Examiner Dr. Jessica Coran must stare into the oldest and darkest instinct known to mankind—murderous rage—to unmask a vicious, phantom killer who leaves his victims in the water, mangled and mutilated. The monster has turned loose his venom against young women in seaside towns and cities along Florida's coastal waters, turning dark the sun. A population is terrorized, unsure when or where the Night Crawler will strike next.

When we talk about chapter outlines at the end of this chapter, we'll show you how Walker develops the first four chapters of this novel in detail.

2. Character Sketches

You need to provide a sense of your main characters' motivations, especially those that will bring the characters into conflict with one another. Most writers simply weave these motivations into the plot summary. Others provide separate thumbnail portraits of their characters.

"The characters' physical descriptions are not vital, but their motivations are," Marilyn Campbell says.

Here's how she describes her *Blood Relations* protagonist:

> Like many successful men who have hit forty-something, Thomas Gage found out how hollow his success really was. By the time Matthew died, Tom was already about to topple. Losing Matthew sent him in the wrong direction: toward disintegration. A second chance with Susan will help to turn him around. He betrayed her love for him when they were young. Now he has to make her believe it isn't too late.

Here's how Peggy Hoffmann describes the heroine for her novel *Wanted: Wife* (Harlequin Temptation):

> Elise Sinclair is in love with love—perfect qualifications for a wedding consultant. From a crumbling Victorian townhouse in Chicago's Old Town, Elise runs her wedding consulting business, A Tasteful Affair. In addition to dealing with tasteless clients, Elise's happiness is hindered by a leaky roof, a temperamental heating system, inconsistent cash flow and two demanding and aloof Persian cats named Clorinda and Thisbe.

She is, Hoffmann tells us, a "hopeless romantic"—a characteristic Hoffmann will reveal in the novel through action and dialogue without ever labeling her.

3. Plot Highlights

Once you've captured interest with an effective hook, you must sustain it with the body of your synopsis. Your hook has made a promise; now you must make good on that promise.

"Detail the beginning and ending scenes and one or two in the middle that give an indication of the kind of emotional intensity or type of action to be expected," Marilyn Campbell says. "Be clear about the type of action in your book. If your story contains explicitly graphic sex or violence, that should be obvious in the synopsis."

"I try to present each major scene in the book by following this form: incident, reaction, decision," Peggy Hoffmann says.

Ah, but which are the major scenes? Here are two guidelines to apply in auditioning a scene for possible inclusion in the synopsis:

1. Do I need this scene to make the primary plot hang together?
2. Do I need this scene for the ending to make sense?

Barbara Parker has a simple rule for picking out plot highlights: "I have gone back to my first rule of novel writing, which is 'How can we make the protagonist(s) suffer?' "

Your synopsis reveals how much and what kind of trouble your poor protagonist is going to encounter. In the next section, you'll learn how to show that in even more detail.

4. Core Conflict

If you don't have a conflict, you don't have a story to tell—or to sell. That's why you need to make sure your book's core conflict is clear in your synopsis.

Ideally, your hook will contain your conflict. In Barbara Parker's "super short spoonful," quoted above, we have protagonist Thomas Gage's double conflict made clear—while solving two murders, he must also confront a past love and the suicide of his only son. In the same way, the opening sentences of John Tigges's synopsis establish an emotional conflict (saving a troubled marriage) and a physical one (the sudden appearance of the monster Sasquatch).

If your conflict isn't implicit in your hook, spell it out. As with your pitch line, you should be able to state your core conflict in a single sentence.

For practice, take a few novels you've read recently and see if you can put the core conflict of each into a sentence.

If you're familiar with these classics of American literature, try the same exercise with each of them:

To Kill a Mockingbird, by Harper Lee
The Old Man and the Sea, by Ernest Hemingway
The Great Gatsby, by F. Scott Fitzgerald
Invisible Man, by Ralph Ellison
Gone With the Wind, by Margaret Mitchell
One Flew Over the Cuckoo's Nest, by Ken Kesey

Did you give them a try? The more you practice, the better you'll get. Here's how we would state the core conflicts for the classic tales.

To Kill a Mockingbird, by Harper Lee: Attorney Atticus Finch fights the bigotry of the small-town South to defend a Black man falsely accused of rape.

The Old Man and the Sea, by Ernest Hemingway: Aging fisherman Santiago battles to save his great catch from sharks.

The Great Gatsby, by F. Scott Fitzgerald: Millionaire Jay Gatsby remains hopelessly in love with his married ex-lover, Daisy Buchanan.

Invisible Man, by Ralph Ellison: Young Black man struggles to define himself in a racist society that insists he deny his authentic self.

Gone With the Wind, by Margaret Mitchell: Headstrong, spoiled Scarlett O'Hara loves her cousin Melanie's husband, Ashley Wilkes, and is in turn loved by the opportunistic and dashing Rhett Butler.

One Flew Over the Cuckoo's Nest, by Ken Kesey: Brash inmate Randall McMurphy fights the oppressive "Big Nurse" in a mental institution.

You'll have an easier time developing and defining your core conflict if you think in terms of one or more of these four traditional categories:

1. person vs. person
2. person vs. nature
3. person vs. society
4. person vs. self

Your core conflict may, of course, overlap categories and could even touch on all four. Here's an example:

Tortured by grief and loss (person vs. self) and fleeing a wrongful conviction for a crime he didn't commit (person vs. society), Dr. Richard Kimble struggles to survive (person vs. nature) while fleeing the relentless lawman who pursues him (person vs. person).

That, of course, states the core conflicts for *The Fugitive*.

If you can't come up with a core conflict to describe your novel, the problem may be with the book rather than the synopsis. Your book must have conflict. If you can't find it, you can't expect an agent or editor to find it, either.

5. The Conclusion

A synopsis is not a quiz or a puzzle. Don't close with a cliff-hanger.

Revealing the ending to your novel won't spoil the story for the editor or agent. It will show that you know how to successfully conclude your plot.

"Make sure every loose thread is tied up, and never leave an editor guessing about anything," Marilyn Campbell says.

"Don't try to be cute and leave us guessing what is going to happen in the story," says editor Karen Taylor Richman. "The whole purpose of this process is to determine if the story is anything that might work for us."

Literary agent Pesha Rubinstein stresses this point. "I cannot stand teasers saying, 'Well, you'll just have to read the manuscript to find out what the end is.' I need to know the whole story in order to see if it makes sense."

If your novel is one of a series, your ending can point to the sequel, as Robert W. Walker does in his outline for *Darkest Instinct*:

> Santiva then tells her about another case he wants her to attend to, one that will take her to London, where a madman is killing people for their eyes. She'll be working alongside the man who helped them track Patric Allain.

HOW TO STRUCTURE YOUR SYNOPSIS

After having worked with editors at five different publishing houses in three different genres—contemporary, paranormal romance and contemporary category romance—Marilyn Campbell says she's learned that "there are no set guidelines for the perfect synopsis."

Develop a format that best lets you tell your story.

Most synopses, especially the shorter ones, weave character and conflict into a tight narrative. Each paragraph must flow naturally from the paragraph before it.

Some writers deal with the conflict in one paragraph, plot highlights in a second paragraph, a paragraph for each major character and then the resolution.

Peggy Hoffmann uses this basic outline for each synopsis.

First paragraph: hook, story setup

Second paragraph: heroine's story goal; motivation; physical description; internal and external conflicts; back story, as needed

Third paragraph: hero's story goal, motivation, physical description, internal and external conflicts, back story

Following paragraphs: story development and conclusion

Carla Anderson, who writes Silhouette romances as Jessica Barkley (*Into the Sunset, Montana Man*), devotes a tight paragraph each to:

> the setting
> the heroine
> the hero
> the beginning
> the romance (internal conflicts)
> the external conflict
> the complication
> the ending

Whatever format you use, if you've enclosed the first three chapters in your submission packet, don't begin your synopsis at chapter four. Let the agent or editor get an accurate sense of your story from the beginning.

FOUR WAYS TO AVOID "SYNOPSIS SPEAK"

Your synopsis is not the place for promotional-style book jacket copy, a medley of adjectives and adverbs, or every possible scene and background detail. But don't settle for a dry plot summary. If your synopsis is flat and stilted, the agent or editor will assume that your manuscript is, too.

Here are four ways to make the synopsis sing:

1. SELECT THE RIGHT TENSE AND PERSON. No matter what choices you've made for the novel itself, write the synopsis in present tense and third person. ("Ahab harpoons the whale.") Third person works well for summary, and present tense creates immediacy and drama.

2. USE AN APPROPRIATE WRITING STYLE. Stick with the same writing style you use in your novel. Dark, brooding novel? You want a dark, brooding synopsis. A chatty, upbeat novel begets chatty, upbeat synopsis.

Dull, plodding novel? Rewrite the novel.

3. WRITE WITH NOUNS AND VERBS. Make strong action verbs and specific, concrete nouns carry the weight. Use adjectives and adverbs sparingly.

Remember, the synopsis is not a book review, and it's not a book jacket blurb. Eliminate opinion words and phrases ("in the next scintillating plot twist, which will have the reader on the edge of the chair . . ."). Just tell your story. Let the editor or agent judge it.

4. USE DIALOGUE SPARINGLY, IF AT ALL. Many successful synopses contain no dialogue. Include dialogue only if it's essential to reveal character or further the plot or create dramatic intensity.

HOW LONG IS LONG ENOUGH?

"The length of the synopsis depends on the complexity of the story's premise, background and motivations," says Harlequin Toronto editor Paula Eykelhof.

"As long as I know where the story is going—the beginning, the middle, the end—I'm not concerned with its length," says editor John Scognamiglio.

But editors and agents agree that shorter is generally better. They want to be able to see at a glance what your book is about.

"I recently heard a great description of a synopsis," says editor Michael Seidman. "Make it read as if you were explaining a movie to a ten-year-old. The more complex you make it, the more holes will open."

Agent Russell Galen looks for about 1,500 words. Karen Taylor Richman wants two to three pages, double-spaced. Editor Jennifer Brehl wants a synopsis of no more than "three pages for the entire book, beginning to end."

A one-page synopsis is often the best bet. It's a chance to show how tight your writing is; it won't put them to sleep; and the shorter the synopsis, the easier it is to refrain from making mistakes.

But a one-page synopsis just won't do the job in many contexts. Your agent or editor might prefer a longer, more detailed synopsis or even a full chapter outline. As in all things, follow our basic philosophy: Give them what they want—no more, no less.

Marilyn Campbell's synopsis for *Pretty Maids in a Row* ran twenty-seven pages in her initial format (because of variances in typesetting, it's a bit shorter here—see pp. 163-180). Too long? It worked, so we'd say it was just long enough.

Elmore Leonard (*Get Shorty, Touch*) took fifteen pages for the treatment for an original screenplay he titled *Legends*. The screenplay didn't sell, but Leonard's agent submitted the treatment as a novel synopsis, and Signet published the book as *Gunsights*. (See pp. 107-114 for a look at Leonard's treatment.)

James Scott Bell provides a marvelous example of the one-page synopsis for his historical fiction thriller *The Darwin Conspiracy* (see pp. 139-140). No synopsis speak here—just good, clear writing. Bell violates our rule that you should always reveal the ending of the novel, choosing to go with a teaser instead. But notice how he reveals plot, weaving historical figures and his fictional Sir Max Busby into a tale of intrigue with scientific and religious overtones.

Following that, Marshall tells all, including the happy ending, in his one-page synopsis for his mainstream novel, *The Year of the Buffalo* (see pp. 140-141). He integrates brief character sketches with plot summary.

ONE-PAGE SYNOPSIS SAMPLE #1

The Darwin Conspiracy (Vision House)

Historical Fiction

75,000 words

by James Scott Bell

What if the theory of evolution was actually masterminded by a cunning atheist bent on ridding the world of God? And what if that atheist left us a manuscript, recently discovered, that laid out the plan in all its crafty detail?

Such a document exists in *The Darwin Conspiracy*, the confession of Sir Max Busby, written in 1926, the year of his death. The account begins with his birth and his relationship with a hateful father, whom Busby eventually murders. It then tracks Busby through an entire lifetime dedicated to seeing evil triumphant.

The insidious Sir Max places himself in the midst of the great events that swayed the world toward evolutionary theory. We start with Sir Max's commission as ship's cook aboard the HMS *Beagle*, which carried the young naturalist Charles Darwin. We follow this relationship up through the publication of *The Origin of Species* and the immediate aftermath. Sir Max also plays a sinister role in Darwin's death.

From there, we see how Busby is instrumental in the "Darwinization" of philosophy, law and theology. Along the way he meets and influences Hitler, Nietzsche, Bertrand Russell and a host of others. But his crowning glory is assisting Clarence Darrow in the Scopes "monkey trial." Sir Max's evil might have gone forever undocumented.

continued on next page

But when he helps to kidnap the evangelist Aimee Semple McPherson, his life takes a truly unexpected turn. He sits down to pen his confession, which exposes the real motivations in the struggle over evolutionary theory.

Intercut with the Busby account is the present-day intrigue surrounding the recovery of the manuscript. When a young attorney is entrusted with it, death and danger are not far behind. Who is trying to stop him? And how far will they go to get the Busby manuscript back?

The Darwin Conspiracy holds the answers. ▲

The Year of the Buffalo (Savage Press)
Mainstream
72,000 words
by Marshall J. Cook

The baseball strike is over, and a season full of last chances begins in Beymer, Wisconsin, the smallest town in America with its own professional baseball team.

Sore-armed pitcher Tommy Lee Smith is about at the end of his minor league career when he joins a collection of young hopefuls and aging hopeless known as The Beymer Buffalo.

Tommy Lee has grown accustomed to a life of long bus rides and empty motel rooms. Beymer will present him with a last chance to find love and a home.

Fewer fans each year have been coming to crumbling Breeze Calhoun Stadium to watch the Buffalo lose. The absentee owner, Hall of Fame pitcher Gordie Glendennon, is ready to move the team to greener outfields (and tax breaks). Beymer can save its Buff, and a large chunk of the local economy, rumor has it, only if attendance reaches 95,000

continued on next page

for the season. That's about double what the Buff have drawn in any of the previous ten seasons.

Tommy Lee immediately feels at home in Beymer, and especially at the Dime-a-Cup Cafe (where coffee is a quarter) on Main Street. Strong coffee and fresh biscuits draw him; a woman named Billie Jo Ferkin offers him a refill. She's at a crossroads, too. The previous owners of the cafe took her in when her truck driver husband forgot to come home from one of his long hauls. Now she runs the place, getting up early to do the baking, closing late to accommodate the insomniacs. That leaves no time for a love life—unless you count a brief and mostly comic flirtation with "Bernie Badgags," the morning man on local station WBEM and public address announcer for the Buff. Tommy Lee might be Billie Jo's last chance at happiness.

Many of Tommy Lee's teammates face their own last chances. Eric Paul "Shave" Posey, once the star closer for the World Champion New York Bombers, struggles with alcoholism. Roy Don "Hammer" Hammond, legendary minor league home run hitter, hangs on for one more shot at The Show. Joseph George WhiteEagle, member of the Ho Chunk Nation, fights to overcome the prejudice that has kept him out of the major leagues. Even Bruce Kelly, the steady second-generation editor of the Beymer Banner, must decide whether his ambitions are ever to extend further than the little town that has been his life.

The Buff get off to a dismal start. But a diving catch that center fielder Will McBride doesn't make triggers the most improbable win in franchise history and turns the Year of the Buffalo around.

On the last day of the season, Beymer wins the pennant and hits its 95,000 attendance goal. Tommy Lee goes to Billie Jo's apartment over the cafe to tell her good-bye. But the words won't come. Instead, he says, "Do you suppose you could make a short-order cook out of me?" ▲

BUILDING YOUR ONE-PAGE SYNOPSIS

In chapter three we revised a query letter to demonstrate how writers can shape and sharpen their work. Now we'll do the same with a synopsis by Kathleen Casey.

Synopsis Checklist

Here is a checklist of elements to look for in the following synopsis drafts and in your own.

_____ Strong lead sentence

_____ Logical paragraph organization

_____ Concise expression of ideas with no repetition

_____ Introduction of main characters—and their core conflicts

_____ Plot high points

_____ Narrative writing in the present tense

_____ Transitions between ideas

_____ Strong verbs

_____ Minimal use of adjectives and adverbs

_____ Correct punctuation, grammar and spelling

_____ The story's conclusion

Read through the original version of Casey's synopsis carefully, noting our suggestions to the author. Then, we'll reveal the final edited synopsis and why it works.

FIRST DRAFT OF SYNOPSIS FOR *SANCTUARY FROM WOLVES*

Sanctuary From Wolves
Historical Novel
by Kathleen Casey

Brandwitha is a Frankish girl who longs for more than her inevitable fate: marriage into a family like hers, where violence and cruelty are commonplace, and the quest for power and wealth is paramount. Her life is a journey toward artistic fulfillment, but the ambition and

continued on next page

betrayal of others made ❶ it a tortuous and dangerous path.

Two travelers happen upon the family villa outside of Paris in A.D. 596. Peter is a priest and teacher from Rome, who stays just long enough to teach Brandwitha to read. Colman is a youth from Ireland who soon travels on to his uncle's monastery, but not before winning her friendship. They both open her eyes to the existence of another world, one of kindness and books. Peter becomes like a father to her, and it hurts her deeply when he leaves for Britain to help found a church. Recognizing Brandwitha's intellect and promise, ❷ he makes her promise him that ❸ she will go into a nunnery.

When Brandwitha is almost a woman, the monk Wolfram teaches her the art of book illumination, but for a terrible price: She must become his concubine. The consequences of their bargain—pregnancy and miscarriage, resulting in sterility—almost destroy her and set into motion her desperate search for a way to both survive and create the art that has become an integral part of her.

This search takes her first to a nunnery in Soissons, where she is content to be a scribe, although she comes to realize she is not devout enough to be a nun. Even here she cannot escape the violent political machinations of the outside world, and she is wrongly accused of treason and cast out.

Alone and afraid in a church sanctuary, the only place she can go, Colman finds her. ❹ As he comes to her aid, their friendship is rekindled. He reluctantly leaves her to go on about his business, fooled into thinking that with his help she will now go to her mother's family in Burgundy. Instead, she makes a dangerous journey to Peter's monastery in England.

continued on next page

1. Should be *make* to maintain present tense.
2. Change the first *promise* to *potential* to avoid the repetition.
3. Delete unnecessary *that*.
4. The introductory phrase seems to modify Colman here.

In the guise of a monk, she realizes her dream of making books, until her sex ❺ is discovered and she is forced to leave.

Once again Colman comes to her—in Dover, where Peter has found a place for her to stay. Colman is on his way home to Ireland to return to his life as a goldsmith, ❻ and has come to say good-bye.

Brandwitha, desperately unhappy where she is, asks him to help her once more and allow her to come with him. She is surprised when he agrees. ❼

In the strange, beautiful land of Leinster, Brandwitha tries to come to terms with her changed circumstances, as Colman tries to show her that there's more than one way to be an artist, and more than one kind of love. Before she can learn this, Brandwitha must make peace with her past—and with herself.

5. *Gender* is more accurate.
6. No change in subject. No comma.
7. Why is she surprised? The author hasn't shown us earlier that she should be surprised. If it's important, this element should come up earlier in the synopsis. If it isn't, leave her surprise out.

Here's our overall assessment: This is very good, very close. We've made a few suggestions about the wording and punctuation. We are concerned, though, that the author too often repeats that Colman leaves the heroine to go about his business. It might be a flaw in the plotting—that he is only available when the author needs him to be. The author must make the reason for his unavailability clearer and avoid the repetition.

The opposite page shows the final draft with our comments, including our thoughts as to why we feel it's a concise, powerful synopsis. Compare the two synopses.

You may disagree with some of our comments and suggestions. That's fine. The important point for you to take away from this exercise is the need to establish character and tone and capture plot—story plus conflict—in a few words.

Sanctuary From Wolves
Historical Novel
by Kathleen Casey

Brandwitha is a Frankish girl who longs for more than her inevitable fate: marriage into a family like hers, where violence and cruelty are commonplace, and the quest for power and wealth is paramount. Her life is a journey toward artistic fulfillment, but the ambition and betrayal of others make it a tortuous and dangerous path. ❶

Two travelers happen upon the family villa outside of Paris in A.D. 596. Peter is a priest and teacher from Rome, who stays just long enough to teach Brandwitha to read. Colman is a youth from Ireland who soon travels on to his uncle's monastery, but not before winning her friendship. They both open her eyes to the existence of another world, one of kindness and books. Peter becomes like a father to her, and it hurts her deeply when he leaves for Britain to help found a church. Recognizing Brandwitha's intellect and potential, he makes her promise him she will go into a nunnery. ❷

When Brandwitha is almost a woman, the monk Wolfram teaches her the art of book illumination, but for a terrible price: She must become his concubine. The consequences of their bargain—pregnancy and miscarriage, resulting in sterility—almost destroy her and set into motion her desperate search for a way to both survive and create the art that has become an integral part of her. ❸

This search takes her first to a nunnery in Soissons, where she is content to be a scribe, although she comes to realize she is not devout enough to be a nun. Even here she cannot escape the violent political

continued on next page

1. We start strong with the core conflict—Brandwitha seeks artistic fulfillment but will face betrayal and danger.
2. Good, clear focus. We learn about Peter and Colman only as they relate to the protagonist and the core conflict.
3. Shows a wealth of conflict and tension. Notice the economy with which Casey narrates all this disaster.

machinations of the outside world, and she is wrongly accused of treason and cast out. ❹

Alone and afraid in a church sanctuary, the only place she can go, Brandwitha is surprised and ashamed to encounter Colman, on a fact-finding mission for his uncle. He is appalled to find her here among thieves and murderers. Colman comes to her aid, at first taking her on as simply a "holy duty." Soon it becomes more, their friendship rekindled as they fight Brandwitha's treacherous family together.

He leaves her to go on about his business, fooled into thinking that with his help she will now go to her mother's family in Burgundy. ❺

Instead, she makes a dangerous journey to Peter's monastery in England. In the guise of a monk, Brandwitha realizes her dream of making books, until her gender is discovered and she is forced to leave.

Peter finds a place for her in Dover, a house of holy women waiting for a nunnery to be built. She is desperately unhappy there but tells herself she cannot expect more. One night, to her shock, Colman comes to see her. He is on his way home to Ireland to return to his life as a goldsmith. He doesn't tell her that he sought Peter out first to learn of her fate: He left his uncle's monastery because of his strong feelings for her, which helped him reclaim his own identity as an artist. Brandwitha only knows that this opportunity is her last chance; although she feels she will be a burden to him again, as well as a stranger in exile, she asks him to allow her to come with him to Ireland.

In the strange, beautiful land of Leinster, as Brandwitha tries to come to terms with her changed circumstances, Colman tries to show her that there's more than one way to be an artist and more than one kind of love. Before she can learn this, Brandwitha must make peace with her past—and with herself. ❻

4. Conflict and tension keep increasing.
5. Now we understand why Colman leaves, opening Brandwitha's life to further conflict.
6. The author resolves the core conflict and reveals the novel's theme without beating us over the head with it. Story must come first; meaning or interpretation, second.

Although we have shown only its first and final drafts for the sake of brevity, this synopsis actually took more than two drafts. You'll probably need several additional drafts to get your synopsis into acceptable shape to send to an agent. It's a lot of work, but it's worth the time and effort you put into it. You'll be thankful for your hard work when an agent calls wanting to represnet your work.

The final draft synopsis provides a model for you to learn from in your work.

THE LONGER SYNOPSIS

Many agents want to see a tight one-page synopsis for your project. The better you get at mastering this challenging format, the more success you're likely to have selling your novels.

But sometimes you'll need a longer synopsis or even a chapter-by-chapter outline. It's always a matter of giving them exactly what they want—no more, no less.

We've provided two successful longer synopses, representing two different genres: romance and mystery.

Six-Page Synopsis

Peggy Hoffmann (writing as Kate Hoffmann) uses a traditional format, weaving plot, character, setting and conflict together into one smooth narrative for her fine romance *Wanted: Wife* (Harlequin Temptation).

Motive and characterization become clear as the author reveals her plot. Notice, too, the double motif. Hoffmann must write knowledgeably about the world of corporate high finance and about a small wedding consulting business.

Her use of terms such as *return on investment* signals the editor that the background will be authentic—a must if the reader is to believe in the characters. Details matter. Even the names of Elise Sinclair's cats help to sell this book.

Wanted: Wife (Harlequin Temptation)
Contemporary Series Romance
By Peggy Hoffmann (writing as Kate Hoffmann)

Wanted: the perfect corporate wife. Impeccable manners, good breeding and a businesslike approach to marriage required. Incurable romantics need not apply. Wedding date three months hence. Send list of qualifications to the Crown Prince of Baby Food, Chicago, Illinois. Jordan Prentiss needs a wife. Not just any wife, but a wife who shares his pragmatic attitude toward the state of holy matrimony.

As one of Chicago's "most eligible," and a brilliant businessman to boot, Jordan's love life is front-page news. But this kind of front-page news isn't good news for the board of directors of BabyLove Baby Foods. They want their president to generate wholesome, family-oriented publicity. When the corporate grapevine forecasts that Jordan will be replaced as president at the next board meeting unless he makes a change in his marital status, the baby food tycoon has to act quickly. He is not about to turn over control of the company his grandfather founded—a company Jordan brought from red ink to a respectable return on investment—especially not to his conveniently married though hopelessly inept cousin.

His strategy? First he must plan the most extravagant wedding Chicago has seen in years. And then he must find a suitable bride.

Timetable for completion? Three months.

Elise Sinclair is in love with love—perfect qualifications for a wedding consultant. From a crumbling Victorian town house in Chicago's Old Town, Elise runs her wedding consulting business, A Tasteful Affair.

In addition to dealing with tasteless clients, Elise's happiness is hindered by a leaky roof, a temperamental heating system, inconsistent cash flow and two demanding and aloof Persian cats named Clorinda and Thisbe.

continued on next page

A die-hard romantic, Elise has always known that one day her prince will come, a man who will sweep her off her feet and rescue her from the day-to-day dilemmas of her life. But eligible single men are in short supply in the wedding business. With no other outlet for her romantic energies, Elise throws herself into planning picture-perfect weddings for her brides and grooms.

When Jordan Prentiss walks in the front door of A Tasteful Affair, without the standard bride-to-be on his arm, Elise thinks that maybe her luck has finally turned. Covered in soot after trying to fix a faltering fireplace, Elise quickly ushers the incredibly handsome Prentiss into her office, only to find that he wishes to enlist her services to plan his wedding.

Though Elise finds it highly unusual that the groom would take responsibility for planning the entire wedding, one look at Jordan Prentiss's no-holds-barred budget dissolves all her doubts. In an attempt to keep word of the wedding out of the media, Prentiss requires that all the details be kept in absolute secrecy. In addition, he tells Elise that to protect his fiancée's privacy, Elise must make all the wedding arrangements through him.

With the income from this job and the publicity the Prentiss wedding will generate, Elise is certain that the job will vault her struggling business into the forefront of Chicago high society. She accepts the job, no questions asked.

Only after she agrees to his terms does Jordan give her the downside. She has just three months to plan this fairy-tale affair for five hundred. It takes only one planning meeting with the bridegroom for Elise to wonder at the romantic fortitude of the future Mrs. Prentiss. She finds Jordan to be aloof, preoccupied and totally disinterested in the details of the most important day of his life. When asked pointed questions about his fiancée's likes and dislikes, he is vague and uninformed, unable to even recall her favorite color. So, in addition to her responsibilities in planning the wedding, Elise vows to try to make Jordan

continued on next page

Prentiss a more sensitive and caring bridegroom. After all, the perfect wedding must have a perfect bridegroom.

As Elise plans the wedding, Jordan begins his search for a bride. With the help of his able executive assistant, Jordan sets off on a quest for the perfect corporate wife. Though many of his girlfriends had been interested in marriage in the past, he immediately eliminates them because of their lofty romantic expectations.

The list of eligible brides is narrowed to five, and Jordan throws a lavish party and invites all five women. When the Crown Prince of Baby Food rejects each of the five prospective princesses, Jordan begins to worry that three months may not be enough time to find a bride. But plans for the wedding continue and the search for a bride goes on.

Soon after, Jordan makes the mistake of telling Elise that his fiancée has not picked out her bridal gown. The schedule-strict Elise is panic stricken. When she once again presses him to involve the bride-to-be, he reluctantly agrees to accompany Elise to a bridal salon to help her choose the dress.

Elise becomes a stand-in bride, modeling dresses for Jordan and secretly fantasizing that she is Jordan's intended. As he helps fit a beaded slipper on her foot, the touch of his fingers sends a jolt of desire through both of them and he kisses her.

Jordan is shocked by his attraction to Elise. Usually controlled and reserved around women, he finds his uncharacteristic behavior and his unbridled reaction too overwhelming to deny. But Elise's romantic expectations of marriage immediately eliminate her as a candidate for bride in Jordan's mind.

Elise, on the other hand, is mortified by her rash behavior and apologizes to Jordan, providing a litany of excuses for the magical moment that seemed to sweep them both away. She comes to the shocking realization that she has been planning her own dream wedding for Prentiss and his mysterious fiancée, and that she is undeniably attracted to her client.

continued on next page

With time running short, Jordan is forced to look at "romantic" persuasion as another weapon to use in his plan to capture a bride. Unfamiliar with the subtleties of courtship, Jordan seeks advice from Elise, asking her to help him become a real Prince Charming to his fiancée.

After their encounter in the fitting room, Elise is confused by Jordan's sudden change in attitude toward his bride. Though she is reluctant to spend more than the necessary time with him, Elise accepts the challenge and showers Jordan with her expertise in romance.

To her surprise, Jordan tests many of her techniques on her, sending her small gifts and flowers and taking her to dinner. Though she is flattered by Jordan's attention, Elise begins to sense that there may be a problem between the bride and bridegroom and guiltily wonders if she is the cause.

As the pair grow closer, Elise starts to discover the man hidden beneath the cool, detached exterior. Though he speaks of love and marriage in very dispassionate terms, she feels that their relationship is moving in a very passionate direction. Elise knows he will be marrying soon, but cannot fight her attraction to him. Jordan doesn't help the situation with his spontaneous kisses and gentle teasing. Faced with a future of unrequited love or a discreet affair, Elise is torn between her growing feelings and her sense of morality.

With just a month and a half left before the wedding, Elise tells Jordan that they must order the invitations. Once again, she questions him on the identity of the bride. Jordan finally admits that there is no bride, at least not as of that minute. He explains his predicament to Elise and asks for her help. Elise is thrilled to find that the man she is in love with is unattached, but dismayed to realize that he has overlooked her as a candidate for bride. The last thing she wants to do is help him in the search for a bride, but she agrees, unable to give up a job that means the future success of her business.

The pair spend more and more time together. One night, the

continued on next page

lessons in love go a bit too far, and both Elise and Jordan are carried away by their simmering passions for each other. Jordan is tempted to ask Elise to marry him, but he knows that he will never be able to make Elise the kind of husband she seeks.

The reality of a lifetime commitment to a woman he doesn't love begins to sink in, and he questions the wisdom in his marrying at all.

Elise knows she is only setting herself up to be hurt, but cannot stand the thought of Jordan marrying another woman. The wedding invitations go out with copy that neatly avoids the mention of the bride's name.

Time is running out, and Elise knows that the magical spell that she and Jordan have fallen under is about to shatter. Elise tells Jordan that she will no longer need his help; the wedding preparations have all been made.

A week before the wedding, Jordan shows up at Elise's door in the middle of the night. Their passions once again get the better of them. But in the aftermath of their lovemaking, Jordan surprises Elise with a proposal of marriage. Though she is tempted to accept, Elise wonders if she is just his last resort in a very desperate situation. She decides not to abandon her romantic ideals, and heartbroken, she refuses Jordan's proposal and asks that he not attempt to see her until the day of the wedding.

For the next week, Elise tries to come to terms with Jordan's impending marriage. She receives word that a bride has been found. When she arrives at the wedding she goes into the bride's room, curious to meet Jordan's choice for a wife. The room is empty. The dress lies across a chair with the beaded slippers beneath.

Jordan appears at the door, dressed in a morning suit and gray ascot. There is no bride, he explains; he couldn't marry another woman when he realized he was in love with Elise. But even though he will lose his company, he has found what it means to love, and he wants to try to make things work between them.

continued on next page

Jordan pushes her into a chair and slips the beaded slipper on her foot, telling her that his princess was right in front of him the whole time, he just didn't recognize her.

Elise tells him to leave her alone and that she will meet him in the church vestibule in fifteen minutes to make the announcement of the wedding's cancellation to the guests. Though she knows she is being impulsive, Elise decides to trust her heart. She grabs the dress and frantically unbuttons the long row of buttons down the back.

When Elise appears in the vestibule, dressed in white and wearing the beaded slippers, Jordan can't believe his eyes. She looks like a dream come true, his dream come true. She tells him that she will pose as his bride to help him save his company. He asks why she would do such a thing, and she admits her love for him. Jordan thanks her for her sacrifice, but tells her that the only way he will walk down the aisle with her is if they walk back as husband and wife. With tears in her eyes at Jordan's romantic declaration, Elise agrees to become his Crown Princess of Baby Food.

As the wedding march sounds from inside the church and the doors to the sanctuary are opened, Elise knows that she has finally found her prince and that fairy tales do come true. ▲

Twelve-Page Synopsis

Agent Diane Cleaver, editor Molly Allen and publisher Bill Grose all gave David Kaufelt suggestions on how to rewrite his proposal for *The Winter Women Murders*, one of his books for his Wyn Lewis mystery series. Kaufelt did the work and won the prize—another brisk seller for Pocket Books. The published product contains a number of "important deletions and additions," Kaufelt says, but the outline sold the book. This synopsis ran twelve pages in Kaufelt's original format.

The Winter Women Murders (Pocket Books)
By David A. Kaufelt

Sophie Comfort Noble, the eighty-four-year-old iron-willed cultural czarina of Waggs Neck Harbor, is found dead in her Bay Street mansion. No one suspects her death is anything but an unfortunate accident.

As a result, her repressed sixty-year-old daughter, Rhodesia Comfort Noble, suffers a breakdown and is persuaded to recuperate by visiting relatives in California. She returns with a new, cosmetically improved persona, her deceased ex-husband's nephew (Peter Robalinski), and a determination to make her mother's pet—and, until recently, extremely local—project—the annual Waggs Neck Harbor Literary Arts Symposium—into a nationally important literary event.

To that end Rhodie directs Wyn Lewis, in her realtor capacity, to get together a list of properties suitable for new Symposium headquarters (now located in a rented office) which would also provide living space for the Symposium's executive director.

Rhodie, clearly unhappy with the direction the Symposium has taken during her absence under the directorship of Jane Littlefield, plans to replace Jane with her nephew. This is not a popular move.

Despite the Symposium's executive committee's disapproval, she settles on the seemingly inappropriate and abandoned cottage on the bay-front lot adjoining her own property.

Researching the cottage's ownership on the village plat maps and in the county tax rolls, Wyn discovers the owner is someone she doesn't know, a W. Bleuthorn of Manhattan. Bleuthorn's attorney's reply that the property is not for sale only strengthens Rhodie's resolve. She directs Wyn to offer a specific and high sum for the cottage, and in the

continued on next page

meantime wants Wyn to find out whatever she can about the history of the property.

When Wyn questions the logic of pursuing the cottage—it's going to need a cellar-to-attic rebuild—Rhodie says that after all it's her money, and it would be nice to have Peter living next door.

Wyn learns from local sources (Ruth and Camellia Cole) that a woman named Mary Bleuthorn (known to Wyn and to most of the village as Poor Mary) owned and lived in the cottage for many years while running the old Main Street Deli. She died in 1968, a year after her daughter won a scholarship to a small school in southern California. The daughter grew up to become Wendy Blue, the sexologist and popular TV personality.

As it happens, Wendy Blue is the real draw of the three principal authors scheduled to speak at the upcoming Symposium, which is devoted to New Directions and Misdirections in Contemporary Feminist Writings. Rhodie is furious, feeling the topic is sensationalistic and decidedly not literary.

Wendy Blue arrives on the Friday morning of the Symposium weekend, takes over the New Federal Hotel bar and, in short order: gives three newspaper interviews; stands up those Friends of the Symposium who have come to greet her by disappearing for an hour; fires Raymond French, her old village playmate and longtime ghostwriter just as his contract is about to pay off for him; gives a local television interview; and snubs Jane Littlefield, Rhodie and one of the other principal speakers, Sondra Goldberg.

Sondra Goldberg is a founding member of the feminist movement, a vocal enemy of Wendy Blue and wife of the critically acclaimed, notoriously henpecked novelist Rupert Hale, obsessive about finally finishing his long-promised magnum opus.

The third speaker, Annie Lee Vasquez, arrives with her twelve-year-old daughter, Caitlin, and immediately hits it off with her host (the

Continued on next page

Friends' Hospitality Committee provides each speaker with an escort, Wyn being assigned to Wendy Blue), Tommy Handwerk. Tommy, Wyn is not happy to observe, responds.

A feminist theme for the Symposium—not to mention such a controversial figure as Wendy Blue giving the keynote address—is a daring Jane Littlefield innovation which has paid off: The Symposium is a sellout for the first time, and every seat is filled in the second-floor library auditorium.

Wendy Blue shocks and titillates and at moments illuminates with her graphic lecture about contemporary female sexuality. During the Q & A, Sondra Goldberg accuses her of "betraying the revolution for profit and neurotic sensuality and destroying the work of women like myself." Sondra says she won't let Wendy Blue get away with it.

Rhodie Noble isn't happy with Ms. Blue, either, and, at the champagne reception after the talk, publicly hands her a check for her honorarium, informs her she no longer has a role in the Symposium and that her escort (Wyn) will be driving her to the airport in the morning.

Like hell, Wendy Blue tells Rhodie Noble, promising—actually, threatening—that she has a few announcements of her own for the morning program and popular consumption.

Wyn decides she's wasted the title company's time asking them to dig out the last title search on the Bay Street cottage: Rhodie's not going to buy Wendy's cottage now, and Wendy's not going to sell it to her. She leaves the gossiping, titillated winter women and goes home to an empty house: Tommy has left a note that he's having a late supper with Annie Lee.

Early the following morning she goes to the New Federal on the off chance that Wendy Blue has decided to pack up her troubles and leave and finds Ms. Blue nude and garroted in her bed, her trademark gardenia turning brown at the edges, covering her pudenda.

continued on next page

Anyone could have come up the back stairs of the New Federal unobserved and killed Wendy Blue, and whoever did took proper precautions against leaving evidence. The village police chief, Homer Price, daunted by past experience with the winter women, not to mention murder, wants Wyn to help.

There are plenty of suspects: Raymond French, whose livelihood Wendy Blue summarily cut off; Sondra Goldberg, seeing herself as the Madonna of the Movement and Wendy Blue as the Antichrist, threatened her in front of a couple of hundred witnesses; Rhodesia Comfort Noble, herself threatened, and not so subtly, by the deceased with revelations now never to come (at least from Ms. Blue).

And probably a great many others, Wendy Blue being infamous for the quantity and quality of her enemies.

Wyn says she really doesn't want to get involved but suggests that Homer get a line on Peter Robalinski, who, for an incoming Symposium director, has not been very visible thus far at this year's events.

At the early Saturday morning Symposium executive committee meeting, it's decided that despite Wendy Blue's murder, the program will continue. Sondra Goldberg, first on the program, ignoring the murder, gives her usual histrionic recreation of the beginning of the woman's movement. Her husband, Rupert Hale, for once does not lead the applause but appears lost in thought.

During the coffee break Rhodie seeks out Wyn and tells her to make new inquiries about the cottage. Now that Wendy is dead, her estate will be more interested in selling. This is characteristically cold blooded, and Wyn is tempted to tell Rhodie to find another realtor; but in the end Wyn, wanting to get out of Waggs Neck and away from the Symposium for a couple of hours, drives over to the West Sea Title Company and has a friend provide access to their computer files.

She discovers that the last title search was completed in 1972 when the property changed hands. This is a surprise; Wyn assumed that Wendy had inherited the cottage when Poor Mary died. Now it ap-

continued on next page

pears that she bought it from a third party.

Further reading of the title search indicates that Wendy did inherit it from her mother in 1970 but almost immediately quitclaimed it to another party for no recorded remuneration. The new owner was Peter Robalinski of Pasadena, California. But according to the plat map, Wendy (that is, her estate) still owns the cottage. Then there is another piece of information Wyn found on the quitclaim deed which gives her pause.

She finds Peter in the Symposium office on Washington Street where he had spent the last month being "shown the ropes" by, and falling in love with, Jane Littlefield.

He explains that he and Wendy were in college together in Pasadena and that she was on a full and rigid scholarship. When her mother died and she inherited the cottage, even though it wasn't worth much, it would have disqualified her from financial assistance. She paid the minimal taxes on it for years and when Peter ran into problems in 1980, he offered it back to Wendy for a price. She eventually agreed to it, though she never forgave him for making her pay for what she had given away.

Wyn has one more question. Why does the quitclaim deed read Wendy Bleuthorn Robalinski? "We were married," Peter admits. "Not that anyone knew, because if the college bursar found out, there would go the scholarship. It lasted two years and then, soon as she graduated, Wendy split, telling me she was going to Mexico for a divorce. When she showed up here on Friday, first thing she did was announce that she had never made it to Mexico."

Later, after the evening session during which Annie Lee Vasquez gave a moving reading of one of her stories (Tommy sitting starry-eyed in the first row), Homer Price finds Wyn and tells her he's got a line on Peter Robalinski from the police in Pasadena. The guy's not Rhodie's nephew.

Oh, Wyn says, beginning to see light.

continued on next page

What's more, he's married. Wyn says she knows, to Wendy Blue. No, Homer says. He was married two months ago in Vegas to none other than Rhodesia Comfort Noble.

Homer Price has no hard evidence, but Peter had a great motive: Killing Wendy would allow him to remain out of jail on bigamy charges and to stay on as Rhodie's secret but nicely set up husband, living just next door in the Mary Bleuthorn cottage, inheriting big time when Rhodie dies.

Homer had planned to detain him but there's a new wrinkle: Sondra Goldberg has been found strangled and nude, not a pretty sight, in her bed, a gardenia covering her pudenda.

Wyn asks if Sondra's husband found her, and Homer says Rupert swears he hasn't been in her bedroom for twenty years. Homer's on his way to question Peter though he can't, for the life of him, think of a single reason why Peter would want to do in Sondra Goldberg.

Wyn, on her way home, finds herself thinking that Jane Littlefield's not a bad suspect for Wendy's murder. She was in love with Peter and was one of those women who didn't feel themselves validated until they were married. She believed Peter was going to marry her, and if she found that he was already married to Wendy Blue. . . .

Tommy arrives home a few minutes after Wyn does, looking very anxious. His mother, Irene, has been in an accident. She was returning on her motor scooter from her night job (Swap & Shop announcer) out at the radio station when an old Mercedes driving on the wrong side of Swamp Road nearly plowed into her. Irene is all right and at home resting, but the Mercedes's driver is in West Sea Mercy Hospital. Rhodie is lucky she didn't kill herself, Tommy says, and Wyn thinks that was probably the idea.

On Sunday morning while the Waggs Neck Literary Walking Tour is in progress and the Symposium is winding down, Homer Price is being kept out of Rhodie's hospital suite by John Fenton, who says Rhodie can't be interviewed for at least another twenty-four hours.

continued on next page

Frustrated, not wanting to go through what might be (from a political point of self-interest) a counterproductive legal procedure, Homer asks Wyn to talk to Rhodie. The case is more or less resolved he says, Peter Robalinski having panicked, leaving last night (Saturday) in the little green sports car Rhodie had given him. Homer has put out an alert and is pretty confident Peter won't get all that far.

Wyn says she can understand why Peter, who's pretty impulsive and not all that bright, might have killed Wendy Blue, but why Sondra Goldberg? Homer explains he didn't kill Sondra, that her husband, Rupert Hale, finally worked up the nerve, trying a copycat murder, failing abysmally, having used one of his bow ties to strangle her, confessing this morning. He is looking forward to prison, he said, where he thinks he has a good chance of writing undisturbed.

Once they find Robalinski the case will be pretty well wrapped. Homer drives out to the hospital again, but Rhodie's got herself discharged and is at home. He calls her from his patrol car and Rhodie, very much in control of herself, tells him that she will see him if she has to but she'd much rather talk to Wyn. She is ready, she says.

Homer, who believes Rhodie has known from the beginning that Peter killed Wendy Blue, agrees, hiring Wyn as a "special" (five dollars per day) member of the department to make it official. His only proviso is that a tape recorder be used and Rhodie, sounding suspiciously insouciant, says, "Why not?"

When Wyn arrives at the Noble mansion on Sunday evening, Peter has already been picked up in Portland, Maine, on his way to Canada. Wyn tells Rhodie he'll be back in Long Island by the next day and charged for murder.

Rhodie, looking like the old Rhodie, sans makeup, dressed in a quintessential winter woman quilted robe, agrees with Wyn that Peter hadn't killed Wendy Blue. Wyn asks if Rhodie had killed Wendy Blue and Rhodie says, quite calmly, that yes, she did. Peter wasn't her ex-husband's nephew but only the manager of the country club out in

continued on next page

Pasadena who had been kind to Rhodie; the first man who had ever showed her affection. They had married, as Wyn knew, but Rhodie hadn't been brave enough to face the winter women with a husband nearly twenty years younger than she. Thus the nephew charade. She had wanted the cottage next door for him. It would have been so convenient. But then it turned out Wendy Blue owned it and was still married to Peter and that Wendy was going to ruin everything.

Poor, naive Peter had met with Wendy on Friday morning when she skipped her meeting with the Friends. He told her about his latest marriage, still believing he and Wendy were divorced. She told him otherwise, and Peter, who was always honest in his dealings with Rhodie, told her. That night, when Wendy threatened to go public with the news that she and Peter and Rhodie were married, in front of all the winter women, Rhodie admits she lost it.

She left the New Federal through its main entry and, getting some picture frame wire from the back of the Mercedes, walked round and took the rear staircase, waiting in the vestibule for Wendy Blue to return to her suite. Wendy invited her in and said there was no way Rhodie could stop her, that she was determined to wring the last drop of fun and publicity out of the situation. "When she turned to remove the gardenia from her hair, I slipped the wire around her neck and really, Wyn, it worked like magic."

Wyn says that Peter must've guessed, and Rhodie agrees. He told her she had to keep quiet, that he was going to take the blame but they'd never find him. When he left, Rhodie says, "I did that fool trick with the car, nearly killing poor Mrs. Handwerk. Lying in that hospital room, I realized that if I killed myself, I was condemning Peter. That's why I'm confessing to you and that little machine."

An expansive Homer Price says, much later, that if Wyn hadn't been doing her usual precise job, going over that title search, Rhodie probably would have gotten away with it. Peter, who is not going to be prosecuted for bigamy, is back in California, a rich man, having

continued on next page

inherited Wendy Blue's estate.

Jane Littlefield has decided not to join him and is more involved than ever with the Symposium, having become very thick with Dolly Carlson. Raymond French is writing a reminiscence of his association with Wendy Blue and is toying with the idea of opening an antique shop on Main Street.

Rhodie has arranged things nicely for herself with some help from John Fenton and a good team of attorneys. She has been declared not of sound mind when she murdered Wendy Blue and is comfortably being held in the private sanatorium which met the state guidelines for her incarceration and which inhabits the two remaining old Mary Immaculate Star of the Sea Catholic Academy buildings (founded by an enterprising Dolly Carlson and a group of down-island psychiatrists). Rupert Hale is in a state facility, happy and productive.

Tommy Handwerk had taken advantage of his open relationship with Wyn to have an open relationship with Annie Lee Vasquez. At the end of the summer, at Lettitia Browne's elegant post-Labor Day parade luncheon in the New Federal's new rooftop cafe for the Friends of the Waggs Neck Harbor Literary Arts Symposium (i.e., the winter women), Tommy reappears, asking Wyn for a closed relationship, asking Wyn to marry him.

Wyn, who has been suffering, tells Tommy she's going to give it some serious thought as she catches sight of Rhodie standing in her rooms on the top floor of the former Mary Immaculate administration building. She wonders how long it will be until Rhodie gets out and whether she will be able to wrest the chairpersonship of the Symposium from Dolly's dictatorial hands. ▲

Twenty-Seven-Page Synopsis

Here's our heavyweight champion—this synopsis ran twenty-seven pages long in Marilyn Campbell's original format (it's shorter here). But it moves—with characterization woven into the action throughout. See if you can stop reading it once you start.

Remember, this is the novel that was turned down fourteen times in its original state. Acting on the advice of her agent, Campbell reslanted and rewrote the whole story. The following synopsis is the result. The ultimate result, *Pretty Maids in a Row*, was a best-selling novel.

"If something more interesting crops up along the way, I never force a story to stick precisely to the synopsis," Campbell admits.

SAMPLE TWENTY-SEVEN PAGE SYNOPSIS

Pretty Maids in a Row (Villard Books)
Mystery/Suspense
By Marilyn Campbell

"I move we cut his balls off and be done with it." Those vicious words are the first Holly Kaufman hears as she enters a hotel suite in Washington, DC, where a meeting is already in progress. Over the years since college, Holly's longtime friend April MacLeash had tried to convince Holly to join The Little Sister Society, but Holly had never been a joiner, and she wanted to forget, not be continuously reminded of the past. She is now thirty-three and a successful environmental lobbyist. A television newscast a few days ago brought the past back with a vengeance, and she gave in to the impulse to call and meet the others that April had told her about.

Already in the suite are four of the five members of The Society. April, who is now an IRS agent, she has known since their freshman year of college, when people kept confusing the two girls because of their appearance. They are both of medium height, with light blond hair, blue eyes and lush figures. April's Tennessee accent and Holly's Pittsburghese quickly differentiate them, however.

Continued on next page

Holly vaguely remembers Bobbi Renquist, a psychologist, whose mousy coloring and demeanor hide a brilliant, analytical mind.

April introduces Holly to Rachel Greenley, a tall, muscular woman who is an agent of the Federal Bureau of Investigation; and Erica Donner, an aggressively competitive redhead who aspires to loftier heights than her present position as vice-president of a major hotel chain. The absent member, Cheryl Wallace, was one of the people featured on the newscast, and thus, could not be present at this meeting.

It was Rachel that had spat out the move for violence. She has been drinking, much to the others' dismay. They have each had to deal with addictions of one kind or another over the years, and Rachel had been clean for some time, but the same newscast that disturbed Holly gave Rachel a push off the wagon. Drinking makes Rachel mouthy—and potentially dangerous. Bobbi explains that the original reason they formed the group back in college was because of what they had in common. After graduation, they agreed to meet twice a year as a sort of self-styled therapy group. Part of recovery is talking about one's problem, both with others who understand from similar experiences and with those loved ones who may have been indirectly hurt because of it.

The women each relate their personal nightmares to Holly. Fourteen years ago, they were all victims of a cruel game perpetrated by eighteen fraternity brothers. The object of the game was for a brother to fill up his "dance card" with as many names of female conquests as possible. It had become a traditional competition in that fraternity, but that year, the contest turned brutal. Seduction and willingness on the part of the girl were no longer necessary. Plying a girl with alcohol and drugs, trickery and rape, by one or a dozen brothers at a time, became acceptable methods of adding names to the cards.

Holly is stunned. She had left school after her ordeal and, not being part of a sorority, had not been aware of how bad it truly was. She had always refused to talk about that time, even when April had urged

Continued on next page

her to. Still not ready to talk about it, she declines to share her tale, but she promises to think about what they've said.

April tells her there's more she can do to heal the pain. Each of The Little Sisters had been victims of the game, until they changed the rules. After they graduated, they were all preoccupied with launching their careers and, in April's and Erica's cases, establishing marriages as well. It took a while to realize that talking to each other was only going so far to help them deal with their problems. Ten years ago, the purpose of The Little Sister Society changed from comfort to revenge, and the results have been most satisfying.

The eighteen men were secretly investigated and tracked, with an eye to finding a way to wreak havoc on their lives. Because of the careers the women had chosen, they were able to exact revenge in a number of ways without having to make any of their identities known. Only a card signed "With the compliments of The Little Sister Society" let the men know their downfall was no fluke.

Timothy Ziegler's appointment to the U.S. Presidential Cabinet changed that. The Society had not been able to find a single flaw in his lifestyle after he left college. All five of the members' names had appeared on his dance card, but Cheryl Wallace had the least to lose by stepping forward to object to his appointment at the confirmation hearings. Public embarrassment would not affect her career as an artist or touch the fortune she had inherited from her family.

Unfortunately, Cheryl was being raked over the coals by several of the Senators and her credibility was waning under stress.

It had been agreed at the outset that Cheryl was the only one who would testify in order to preserve the secrecy of The Society. They still had important work to do, and besides, the way the hearing was progressing, it was beginning to look like Ziegler's appointment would be confirmed, even if twenty women testified against him.

Holly admits that her name would have been on Tim's dance card also. That was why the newscast was so upsetting. But he was not the

Continued on next page

one who had set her up for a trip to hell. She asks the women if Jerry Frampton was one of the eighteen boys, and what, if anything happened to him.

April tells her his is one of the five names left on their hit list—not because he's been squeaky clean like Ziegler, but because he's such a sleazebag. He's now the publisher of a men's magazine, and disgusting secrets that have been revealed about him, past or present, have only made him and his magazine more popular. Nothing he's done has landed him behind bars, however. Even his financial records appear to be in order.

Rachel suggests they turn his file over to Holly. A new tidbit of information had turned up that she hadn't had time to track down. All Holly would have to do is leak it to one of the hungry reporters she knows in Washington, follow that person's progress, then report back to Rachel. Holly is hesitant, but they talk her into at least taking Frampton's file and reading it over—for her own good. They also give her the three other names on the list besides Frampton and Ziegler in case she learns anything of interest about them. She scribbles the names on the inside of the folder, but doesn't agree to do any more than look at the reports inside.

From a chair in the hotel lobby, investigative reporter David Wells had watched four professionally dressed women between the ages of thirty and thirty-five enter the private elevator to the penthouse suite within a half hour of each other. Two hours later, the same four come down, one at a time. David had been trying for two days to interview Erica Donner, the vice-president of the corporation that owns this hotel and a string of others. He was only attempting to get some details for an article he was working on about the latest buyout she was negotiating, but her evasive tactics caused his nose to twitch. Since she refused his request to meet with her, and having nothing more pressing to do that day, he had decided to hang out in the lobby in hopes of catching her on her way in or out.

continued on next page

As the fourth woman exits the elevator with a slight stagger, his curiosity is piqued. He follows the woman to the building that houses the Federal Bureau of Investigation, but loses her after she goes inside. Exuding a considerable amount of his boyish charm on a female guard gets him the woman's identity: Special Agent Rachel Greenley.

He has no idea why an FBI agent would have been meeting with Erica Donner, and he doesn't yet know the identities of the other three women. But his reporter's instincts tell him there's a story here.

After the meeting broke up, Holly went for a long walk rather than return to her office near the hotel. She needs time alone to digest everything she's learned. Listening to those women brought back every detail of what Jerry Frampton did to her . . .

She was a nineteen-year-old sophomore, an outstanding student and a shy virgin. Jerry Frampton had slithered into her life in the guise of a jock who needed tutoring. After all his other efforts to have sex with her failed, he talked of marriage and forever. Naive child that she was, she believed him. Her mother had convinced her that her virginity was a special gift from God. It could only be given away one time, and she should be absolutely certain the recipient was deserving of the honor. She decided Jerry was the man she had been waiting for, the one she would give the ultimate gift of her love.

At the end of their next date, Jerry talked her into playing a game. He wanted to see if shutting out two of their senses would enable them to communicate mentally. She assumed it was another of his attempts to get her into bed with him, but, since that was her intention that night anyway, she went along with him. Blindfolding her before they entered her apartment, Jerry made her promise to abide by a no talking rule. He led her into her windowless bedroom, where it was so dark the blindfold was unnecessary.

The night became a sensuous journey into womanhood for Holly. The next morning, however, after switching on the light, she turned

continued on next page

to awaken her future husband with a kiss—and froze in shock.

The naked lover in her bed was a stranger.

Before she could gather her wits, someone pounding on her apartment door demanded attention. The early morning visitors were Jerry and one of his fraternity brothers. Suddenly she remembered having seen the man in her bed before—at Jerry's frat house. His name was Tim Ziegler. On the edge of hysteria, Holly managed to absorb the fact that she was the victim of a fraternity prank.

Jerry was so furious with her for putting out to Tim instead of him, he hit her, then shoved her down on the floor, intending to get what he deserved. Tim made an attempt to stop him, but the other brother dragged Tim out of Holly's apartment so that Jerry could rape her in peace.

The pain has not lessened in fourteen years. The inhuman treatment by the college counselor and security people she had complained to and the cruel taunts and subtle threats of her classmates in the days that followed had been more than she could cope with. She had quit school and gone home to her parents. Bernie and Vivian Kaufman had never insisted she tell them what had happened to drive her away from school, even when she inflicted on them her depression, temper tantrums and tranquilizer addiction. Foolish or not, she was afraid that, like the others, they would believe she had somehow been at fault. Holly recalls the advice Bobbi had given her about discussing the incident and decides the time has come to have a long overdue talk with her parents. Perhaps if she could make amends with them, she could begin to forget. Before she can lose her nerve, she heads home to Pittsburgh on the next airline flight. She should have known what their reactions would be to her story, but self-doubt had blinded her. As the only survivor of three children, Holly has always been the center of the universe to them. She finally realizes she didn't tell them before for fear of losing that cherished position. Instead of blaming her for poor judgment, they respond as if they had been stabbed in the heart

continued on next page

that very day.

Vivian cries and shares the heartache of her daughter's lost innocence. Bernie vows to kill both the bastards who hurt his baby, or at least castrate them. He seems sincerely disappointed when Holly tells him she doesn't want him to do anything on her behalf.

The visit lifts one of the weights from her conscience and convinces her there is another person she owes the same consideration as she gave her parents—Philip Sinkiewicz, her employer, friend and onetime lover. Holly met Philip and his wife, Cora, while working in her parents' restaurant after she had moved home. They were friends of her parents and closer to their age bracket than Holly's. One evening, Philip drew Holly into a conversation that gave her the final shove back into the real world. Philip had finally secured the funding he had been seeking to establish Earth Guard, an organization devoted to political lobbying for environmental concerns. He informed Holly that the fledgling lobby would be needing all the help it could get from intelligent, young people. They would have a place for her if she would like to move to Washington, DC. Within a week she had decided to take him up on his offer.

Philip and Holly spent a great deal of time together setting up Earth Guard. His zealousness about saving Earth's resources was contagious, and she soon found herself caught up in his interests as well as the fast-paced life of the Capitol. He recognized her genius and untapped talents and urged her to finish college in order to give herself every advantage in the competitive city. She chose a school in the DC area so that she could continue to work with him.

As the years went by she realized his feelings for her went beyond that of a close friend and employer, but he never acted upon his obvious desire. He was a man who took his wedding vows seriously, regardless of how difficult that marriage was for him. Even if he had not been married, however, Holly never wanted another man in her bed.

About seven years ago, Philip's wife was diagnosed with cancer of

continued on next page

the brain. For two years he suffered along with her as she underwent surgery and treatments, unspeakable pain and forgetfulness. As his closest friend, Holly was always there for him and shared his every frustration. Understanding Philip's confusion of grief and relief after Cora's funeral, Holly cared too much to add to his distress by denying him the comfort he sought in her arms. Temporarily setting aside her vow of celibacy, she spent the night with him, but learned that compassion and friendship are not sufficient motivation for physical lovemaking. Either that, or her ability to enjoy the experience was killed the morning after she had discovered it.

That loss, and the inability to return the love of a man as wonderful as Philip, compounded her hate—and her guilt. She had done her best to put it behind her and had almost convinced herself it didn't matter. Bobbi may have been right when she said, "A rape victim tends to continue to be a victim until she learns to fight back."

Holly goes directly from the airport to Philip's home. After that one time, she turned down his gentle hints to repeat the intimacy, but that never seemed to bother him. Over the years, he was always respectful and attentive, clearly devoted to her and no other woman. He often tells her how much he loves her and, once a year on the anniversary of their night together, he asks her to marry him, or at least share his home.

But she likes things the way they are. Without relinquishing her independence or privacy, she has a good friend to be her escort when she needs one and to act as a buffer between her and other men. Philip may want more, but he has never demanded anything beyond being her steady companion. Knowing that he has no competition for her affections seems to be enough for him.

She realizes there is a good chance that he might one day run into Ziegler, and Philip might feel the need to say something embarrassing to them all. Therefore, she tells Philip a vague version of her experience without revealing exact details or the names of the boys.

continued on next page

Philip's face contorts with rage, and for a moment Holly fears he is angry with her, but he calms down almost immediately and expresses his sincere sympathy. Philip now understands her fear of the dark, the way she jumps when someone touches her unexpectedly, her distrust of men and her distaste for sex. He wishes he could send the men involved to perdition for the damage they did to such a sweet, innocent girl, and for preventing her from having a normal relationship with him. He loves her all the more now that he's aware of the reasons behind her behavior.

He gives her a hug and an undemanding kiss, then asks her where she's been all day. She tells him about the reunion with some women she knew in college and her unplanned visit with her parents. He is sorry she didn't let him know about that, since he would have enjoyed seeing Bernie and Viv also. He says he will have to give them a call. Before leaving, she goes to the bathroom and, as she walks back into the room, she sees Philip thumbing through the folders in her briefcase. When she questions him, he scolds her for taking too much work home.

Two days later there is an announcement on the news that Timothy Ziegler's appointment has been confirmed. Cheryl Wallace had not convinced the Senate Committee that he should be disqualified. Someone watching the broadcast is furious with the turn of events. This person determines to personally punish Ziegler for his crimes of years ago.

The next day, David Wells is having lunch with his friend and mentor, Harry Abbott, when a gorgeous blond and an older, white-haired man enter the deli. Not only does the woman catch David's attention because she has all the attributes he is normally attracted to, but he remembers her from the hotel. He hasn't been able to let go of the feeling that there's a story right under his nose that no one else knows about.

David pretends to recognize the man to wrangle an introduction, but he is very protective of his lady. And the lady never once meets

continued on next page

David's eyes. David is not foiled, however. He sees the name on the man's charge card—Philip Sinkiewicz—and knows what to do with that. One phone call to the newspaper's society columnist, Christine Manning, gets him more information than he needs. It also gets him invited to a fund-raiser dinner where Christine is certain Holly and Philip will be the next night.

Christine tells him of Holly Kaufman's reputation for shooting down would-be suitors. If he wants to get close to her for any reason, it will have to be through Philip and for business purposes only. David's well-known seductive skills will get him nowhere with her, but Christine is anxious to watch him try.

As Christine predicted, Holly seems immune to his smile, but responds to the bait of an article about Earth Guard. By the end of the evening, they have an appointment to meet at her office.

Until that night, Holly had avoided picking up Frampton's file. The same reporter turning up twice seemed a strange coincidence, and she recalls Rachel's suggestion that she turn the Frampton lead over to a hungry reporter, then follow his progress. It sounded easy enough, and the information in the file certainly warranted such action.

A knee injury ended Jerry Frampton's promising football career, and his limited talents narrowed his choices for the future. He has since become the publisher of a popular men's magazine focusing on sports and nude women. The last notation in the file states that it has just been discovered that during the time when he was launching his magazine, Jerry Frampton had been closely associated with Mick Donley, a convicted child pornographer. If Frampton still had his fingers in the pie of the illegal side of smut, it could finally mean his ruin.

As Holly goes to sleep, someone enters the Ziegler bedroom and places ether-soaked cloths over Tim's and his wife's faces. When the intruder is certain they will not awaken too quickly, a gag is stuffed in Tim's mouth, and he is stripped. The intruder then hauls the naked,

continued on next page

unconscious man out into the backyard and ties him to a tree, upright. When Ziegler comes to, he is told it's payback time. He doesn't understand until his captor picks up a large pair of hedge clippers from the ground. Ziegler's muffled screams and pleading eyes do not slow the progress of the blades of the giant scissors as they are positioned on each side of his genitals, then swiftly brought together. As Timothy Ziegler's lifeblood drains from his body, a sign is hung around his neck with stick-on letters that read:

JUST PUNISHMENT FOR A RAPIST

The next morning the news is filled with speculation about the reported murder of the just-confirmed Secretary Ziegler. The police are not releasing details, other than that it was a home invasion, and the wife and children are in seclusion.

Rachel Greenley is informed by her superior that she will be part of the task force working with the local police on Ziegler's murder. She can barely constrain her laughter at the incredible irony of it all. Holly was upset by the way the hearing ended, but she still feels sympathy for the wife and children. The hearing itself had to have been a difficult ordeal for them, but this was so much worse.

Before her meeting with Wells, she checks on him through a friend. David Wells is an up-and-coming journalist, hungry and aggressive, yet scrupulously honest with his stories. Gossip has it that he has cut a wide swath through the female population of DC, but shows a decided preference for buxom, blue-eyed blonds like herself. That could make dealing with him difficult, but, other than that, he sounded perfect for what she was planning to do. If Earth Guard got some publicity out of it at the same time, so much the better.

When David requests a postponement of their appointment until dinner, Holly hesitantly agrees. Throughout dinner, they interview each other. She asks several questions about where he gets his leads and how he decides what tips to investigate. He eventually questions her about what she was doing at the hotel last week and she refuses to

continued on next page

say more than "meeting some friends." He does learn that she is leaving in a few days for a three-week tour of the United States. She will be addressing city governments about taking advantage of new environmental conservation laws and how to apply for grants to get started. David senses she is playing with him, and his charm becomes a weapon to demonstrate his greater experience with the game. Before they part, he lures her into a seductive kiss, then insults her.

Holly is shocked by his ability to arouse feelings she believed were dead, but has no intention of experimenting further. His devastating kiss and well-aimed insult make Holly realize she is no match for him. She backs away, intending to find another, more malleable instrument of the press.

David is somewhat shocked at his own ill-mannered behavior with Holly. Everything about her aroused and annoyed him simultaneously. He figures he owes her an apology, but he has a dislike for telephone communication, besides having a personal rule against using it with women he's interested in. And he's definitely interested in Holly Kaufman. Besides intriguing the hell out of him, he knows she has a secret or two, and the meeting at the hotel has something to do with it. He tells himself if he pursues her, it will be mainly because of that secret and not because she holds any special attraction for him.

David has moved up through very traditional ranks. One of five children raised by an overburdened father whose laborer wages were supplemented by welfare, David's first job was a newspaper route. Later he got hired as a copy boy and was taken under the wing of Harry Abbott, a tough-talking, softhearted sportswriter. With the help of a newsboy scholarship David worked his way through college. For years his pieces were relegated to the middle pages, but he has recently risen above the mediocre by uncovering a scandal in the Department of Housing and Urban Development. A good-looking, thirty-five-year-old bachelor with a charismatic personality, David is accustomed to

continued on next page

making feminine conquests with little more than a wink and a grin. Women quickly discover his intention to remain single, but that knowledge does not deter their vying for his companionship, and even seems to make him more sought after.

David's mother taught him at an early age not to put his trust in the female gender. She walked out on her husband and brood of young children and never looked back. David enjoys women, but abides by the advice Harry Abbott gave him: "When you're up to bat, go for a homer, and when you're not, play the field."

Tim Ziegler's murderer is disappointed at first by the lack of information made public, but decides it could be beneficial. The next execution will take a little longer to plan. After that one, they will know Ziegler was not an isolated incident and they won't be able to keep it quiet. The world must be shown what a rapist's punishment should be. In the meantime, it will be interesting to see if Holly comes up with anything substantial on Jerry Frampton before the plan is in place.

David convinces his boss that he's onto something big and gets himself assigned to cover Holly's tour that begins on the West Coast then meanders eastward. After that, it's a simple matter to reserve the seat next to her on the long flight. At first Holly is very upset at seeing him. His sincere apology makes her feel somewhat better, but when he reveals his very real terror of flying and she is able to help him through it, the tension between them rapidly dissipates. Within a few days however, a new kind of tension has built between them. Only hours of raw, passionate sex, the likes of which Holly had no way of knowing about, satisfy their mutual needs.

More surprising is that they actually grow to like each other

continued on next page

as well. Nevertheless, they both assume this is a temporary infatuation that will go away once they're back in Washington. After they return, thinking he is in danger of falling under Holly's spell, David stays away from her for several days. He must continually fight his own desire to pick up the phone and at least talk to her, but that in itself tells him how close to the edge he got with her.

Holly is both angry that he could set her out of his mind so easily and relieved that her one detour into passion's parlor is over. She tells herself it was an interesting experience, but now her life will return to its normal, predictable state. She's proven wrong when she enters her office one morning to find David waiting for her. They both know instantly that the fire between them is still raging.

A few minutes later, Philip comes into Holly's office to speak to her. Although she and David are across the room from each other, he suspects something. David cannot resist letting Philip know that he had covered Holly's tour. After Philip leaves them alone again, Holly berates David for pulling such a macho trick, but he's as angry with himself as she is. When he explains he's never been jealous before and didn't realize how stupid it could make him, she forgives him and agrees to meet him for lunch. Philip confronts her the moment David exits. His own jealousy is barely contained as he warns her about what a womanizer David Wells is. She should know better, he reprimands her. She's already been damaged by his kind. Not ready to admit there is anything serious between her and David, and not wanting to hurt Philip, she tells Philip that she is only talking to David because of the article he's doing on Earth Guard. Philip wants to believe her badly enough that he accepts what she tells him.

At lunch, Holly decides to give David the information on Frampton, without revealing how she came upon it. The reminder that she is still keeping secrets irks him, but he takes the bait and is soon headed out of town again. While he is gone, Holly goes out to dinner with Philip, fully intending to tell him about her relationship with David.

continued on next page

Before she can begin however, he lets her know how badly she could hurt him if she ever left him and how worried he was about her involvement with Wells. Seeing his very real distress, Holly decides to wait a little longer before telling him. After all, this whole thing with David could go away in a few weeks, and she would have broken Philip's heart for nothing.

What David expects to be a preliminary fact-finding trip to Florida becomes a dangerous interlude with the pornographer, Donley. David ends up being the key figure in a deadly FBI sting operation to arrest Donley and confiscate his illegal films. The feature movie of the collection is a snuff film in which a prostitute was beaten to death. What makes it doubly valuable is the moment when the camera focuses on a familiar face, a man who had been offstage until he realized the actor had gone too far. The face belongs to Jerry Frampton. He was an accessory to murder.

During Holly's weekly phone conversation with her parents, her father tells her he is gratified that Ziegler is dead and Frampton's been arrested, but it will be even better if he gets the electric chair. Holly is taken aback by his extreme bitterness when her own has been diminishing with every one of David's kisses. When he asks how things are going between her and Philip, she promises to talk to him about that at another time. She knows her father would be extremely happy and relieved if she would marry Philip and "settle down."

David comes home after his near brush with death, ready to make a commitment to Holly. Just as they admit their love for one another and they are taking their relationship to a deeper level, the telephone rings. Holly decides to let the answering machine pick it up, never imagining it could be anything she wouldn't want David to hear. Unfortunately, it's April, calling to congratulate Holly on a job well done and for picking the perfect reporter for the job.

The only way Holly can explain is with the whole truth, but David feels too betrayed to listen rationally. They end up having a fight about

continued on next page

the definition of rape and Holly orders him out of her life.

One disappointment is followed by another. Jerry Frampton gets off due to a technicality. But one person sees it as a sign to strike again. On his way home, Frampton is abducted and brutally butchered, just as Ziegler was. This time details of the murder are revealed plus the similarity to the Ziegler case. It is assumed that a psychotic, militant feminist is at large.

Holly is badly shaken by the news. She calls April to be reassured that no one in The Little Sister Society could be behind the murders. She remembers Rachel's sarcastic comments about castration and how April said the woman was dangerous when she was drinking. April tells her she meant Rachel is dangerous to herself and nothing The Society has ever done was illegal. Hours later, Holly receives a call from Rachel. Her words are terribly slurred as she tells Holly she's spoken with April and heard she was worried. Rachel would never have approved bringing Holly into their group if she had known she was such a coward. She threatens Holly, saying if she tells anyone about The Society or repeats anything she heard, they'll do to her what they've done to men.

David goes to see Holly only to order her to go to the police about the women she met with. They are both still angry with each other, but she tells him about the threatening call from Rachel. Since she doesn't really have any proof against her, she doesn't dare go to the authorities. He informs her that, in that case, he's going to do it for her.

Seeing her again makes David realize that he's far from getting over her, but after making her secret public, he's certain she'll hate him enough to guarantee that their relationship will never stand a chance. He goes back to his contact at the FBI and makes them a deal. They get his solid lead on the two murders in exchange for first crack at a breakthrough in the cases. Also his request is granted to have an agent assigned to protect Holly until the whole matter is settled.

Another shock wave hits Holly when April calls to inform her that Rachel committed suicide after being questioned by her superior in

continued on next page

connection with the murders. Her farewell note said she "couldn't live with the shame or guilt any longer." She never confessed to killing the two men, but Holly assumes that was the guilt she spoke of in her note. The FBI is not so sure. Agents begin questioning the other women of The Little Sister Society. They are all frightened and suspicious now. It is mentioned more than once that the murders never began until Holly Kaufman joined The Society and the two men who were killed were the ones who had raped her.

The FBI turns most of their attention to Holly, but they have nothing substantial to arrest her on. Philip is beside himself with worry for her, but he must go out of town for a day or two. He'll stop by as soon as he returns to make sure she is fine. He promises her everything will turn out all right. David returns, distraught over way things twisted around against her. He knows she's not capable of murder. He also knows he loves her and wants to try to make it work between them.

That night, the third man named on The Society's list, William O'Day, is murdered by the same method. This time, Holly has an airtight alibi—David spent the night with her, and there was an FBI agent watching her apartment. Philip shows up the next day and is shocked to find David with Holly in an obviously intimate situation. He leaves, but his hurt expression breaks Holly's heart, because she knows she should have been honest with him much sooner. They are speculating about who could be behind the vicious murders when Philip returns and politely asks to come in. Once inside he pulls a gun on them. David tries to talk him out of doing anything foolish, since he was undoubtedly observed coming in by an agent. But Philip doesn't care what happens to him now that he knows Holly will never be completely his. All these years he had to accept the fact that she couldn't give him all of herself. All these years he believed that she belonged to him and only him, and that one day she would be his in every way, but he never understood what held her back. It all became clear the day she told him about her abusive treatment by "two college

continued on next page

boys," and how they had gone unpunished for their crimes. As long as they were alive and free men, she didn't feel truly safe. That was when he realized what he had to do to make things right between them. He had to punish them himself. He had seen the list of names in the odd folder she had with her that day. It was easy to get the names of the two boys from her father, then check them against the list. The rest was just piecing facts together. He punished Ziegler and Frampton for her. Then when he saw that the authorities were accusing her, he killed O'Day to draw their attention away. After all, her grudge was with the first two, not the last one. Philip had ascertained that all five men on the list in her folder were fraternity brothers, so it could be assumed that O'Day was a rapist, too. Therefore, his punishment was justified. He did it all for her, to make the past go away so that she could come to him as his woman. He had believed her when she said nothing was going on between her and Wells, but he shouldn't have. She didn't have the experience to deal with the tricks of a snake like Wells. He, Philip, had paid the price, but Wells has stolen his reward.

Philip points the gun at David and fires at the same time David dives for cover behind a sofa. Before he can pull the trigger again, Holly throws herself against Philip, knocking him to the floor. She refuses to be a victim any longer. Before Philip absorbs the fact that Holly has turned against him, the FBI agent bursts in, having heard the shot. Philip shoots at the man, hitting his arm, but the agent already had his gun ready and pulls the trigger. The bullet strikes Philip between the eyes.

David and Holly know they have a long way to go to put their individual pasts behind them, but they both believe it will be easier if they work on a new beginning together. ▲

REWRITING YOUR SYNOPSIS TO SPECIFICATION

Sometimes, instead of a solid yes or no, your synopsis will earn you a "maybe, if. . . ." If an agent or editor offers suggestions, pay attention. Any guidance you get here will be more relevant and useful than any you could receive from a critique group, book doctor or writers conference. Your willingness to rethink and rewrite a synopsis just might sell your novel.

Robert W. Walker had done one book with an editor and then had struggled for nearly five years to sell another title to "the only company in Publication Land who'd ever purchased a thing from me."

He was nearly crushed when the proposal for a book to be called *Downfall* got rejected. So he telephoned the editor and asked why he'd been turned down (something we usually advise against doing).

"Two reasons," he remembers her replying. "We're doing long books now, not short. Our novels have to be at least 80,000 words, and that leaves *Downfall* 20,000 words short."

And reason number two?

"We're full up on mysteries right now. What we really need is more horror scripts," she replied.

"All right. Give me a contract, and I'll add 20,000 words and put in a monster."

She agreed, and Walker had a sale. That's flexibility.

When David Kaufelt finished his proposal for *The Winter Women Murders* and sent it along to his agent, Diane Cleaver, she had "incisive and important comments," he reports.

Using those comments, Kaufelt rewrote the proposal and sent it to Molly Allen, his editor at Pocket Books. She also had "important and incisive comments," he says, so he rewrote the proposal yet again.

That version went to the publisher, Bill Grose, "who had very incisive and very important comments," Kaufelt says.

One more rewrite, and the proposal was accepted by agent, editor and publisher.

Kaufelt says he goes through the same process with each of his Wyn Lewis mysteries. The result of this creative collaboration has been a popular series—first, because Kaufelt works hard at his craft, and second because he's willing, even eager, to accept guidance from pub-lishing professionals.

Marilyn Campbell offers an experience that emphasizes the wisdom of the rewrite even more strongly.

Fourteen editors rejected her novel *Pretty Maids in a Row* in its original state, she reports, "although it was that version that landed me my agent because she believed in its potential."

After a year of shopping a synopsis and 250 pages of text, Camp-bell's editor on a previous project, *Come Into My Parlor*, suggested she come up with an entirely new slant to tell her story. Campbell went right to work, created a new synopsis, and made a sale before she even rewrote any of the actual manuscript.

"Twenty-four hours after that deal was made," Campbell adds, "Villard Books, a division of Random House, bought the hardcover rights to *Pretty Maids*, also based on the revised synopsis only."

Your synopsis is an important marketing tool, and a revised synop-sis, incorporating suggestions from editors and agents, can make the critical difference between rejection and publication.

THE CHAPTER OUTLINE

Everything we said previously about the style and tone for your synop-sis applies also to the chapter outline. Now, however, you'll go into much more detail, describing the plot chapter by chapter. More detail doesn't justify wordiness, though. Just as with the synopsis, you don't want one unnecessary syllable in anything you send out.

Robert W. Walker used a twenty-seven-page, twenty-two-chapter outline to sell *Darkest Instinct*. We've included the first four chapters of this outline here to show you how he captures the novel's excite-ment while spelling out its structure.

Darkest Instinct
by Robert W. Walker

CHAPTER ONE

Opens on April 2, 1996, with a pair of shark research trainees for the University of Florida's Abbott Laboratory in Islamorada Key, Florida, shoving dead sharks onto a conveyor belt. Ironically, in order to get enough specimens to study the procreation cycle of the shark, the facility has just completed a three-day "Shark Research Fishing Tournament." Inside, on the dissecting tables, Dr. Joel Wainwright has discovered an inordinate number of human body parts within the digestive tracts of the sharks so far collected and opened up. One body part in particular has disturbed Dr. Wainwright and his colleagues, so he has called in the FBI as a result.

Wainwright faces down the wrath of his superior who had wished to keep outside agencies at bay, but he is willing to take the heat, since he is a man of ethics and principles. What he has uncovered indicates a recent murder victim who has been "fed" to the sharks.

CHAPTER TWO

FBI Medical Examiner Jessica Coran and her new boss, Eriq Santiva, Chief of the FBI's Criminal Profiling Division IV, fly to Miami from Quantico through a terrible blizzard and turbulence by commercial air on their first leg toward out-of-the-way Islamorada Key where they hope to see firsthand what Dr. Wainwright has. Along the way, Santiva is continually ill over air travel. It doesn't help his stomach when, on the flight down, Jessica insists on going over the police files and M.E. protocols on a number of young female victims who've washed ashore on Florida's otherwise serene and lovely sun-drenched beaches. In some cases, sharks have taken their toll on the bodies, so when the call had come from Wainwright, Jessica and Santiva were understandably interested and anxious to follow up. From Miami, they helicopter

continued on next page

to Islamorada Key where Jessica tells Santiva that he may as well rent a car and find a fishing boat and get out of her way, because she will need at least twenty-four hours, and possibly more, with the hoard of body parts collected and refrigerated by Wainwright. They learn something of the research being carried out here along the way. This is when Wainwright shows Jessica one body part in particular with a shark-bitten gold chain embedded in the wound. It takes some effort to remove the thin, fragile chain intact, but Jessica meticulously does so, and she finds a startling revelation. The chain is engraved with a single, simple word: Precious. It is an endearment which the daughter's father, a congressman, has always used for Allison Norris, the most recent victim—the dead girl in the police photos Jessica viewed on the plane coming down.

CHAPTER THREE

This chapter is framed by the present situation in Islamorada Key where Jessica sets about working, but within the frame, she recalls all that she has learned about the victims, the killer, Santiva and his ability with handwriting analysis which he showed her on the plane coming down. This establishes that they have a strange handwritten note from the killer, longhand, a note which the reader sees (in longhand, not typed); Santiva explains why they believe the note—a poem—is genuine. It is signed with the symbol of the tau cross. Santiva explains that if it's not the killer's work, it is still from an extremely disturbed and psychotic second. Such dark poetic notes in longhand will continue throughout the book. The chapter ends with Jessica continuing her work at the lab in the Florida Keys.

[Walker provides a copy of the handwritten note here.]

CHAPTER FOUR

This chapter, set in two scenes, shows the killer and his methodical approach to gain the acceptance and trust of his victims. He is smooth,

continued on next page

charming as a cobra, his money and obvious wealth adding to his allure. The chapter introduces Tammy Sue Sheppard and her two friends who are out on the town, having drinks and enjoying the moon over Miami when Tammy is whisked away by the killer, literally swept off her feet. He takes Tammy to his boat while her girlfriends look on with jealousy and frustration. Cynthia pretty well gets over it and tries to ignore the situation, but Judy has a sense of foreboding, an ill at ease queasiness at watching her friend disappear with the handsome stranger, coupled with a healthy desire to see Tammy's evening spoiled, but she fails to act on these impulses.

Scene two chapter four has Tammy aboard, and they are now far out on the water, the lights of Miami a few twinkling blinks. In the throes of passion one moment and fighting for her life the next, Tammy is vividly shown her fate before she dies when the killer reveals other victims in various stages of decay tied by rope at the back of his launch. And Tammy does not die quickly or easily as the killer strangles her only up to a point, reviving her to play out her death several times, and then he finally ties her by the neck and places her gently into the ocean and drags her alongside other bodies there behind his boat which he has named after the T cross as *The Tauto*. The killer is a sociopath with a bizarre fantasy involving the tau cross. His particular fixation fantasy is gone into in more detail as the story unfolds. ▲

CHAPTER
SEVEN

CRAFTING THE COVER LETTER

"Some publishers go to great lengths to talk about what the cover letter ought to say, but we don't publish cover letters. We publish stories."

—Kent Brown, Boyds Mills Press

Y ou're almost ready now to send your synopsis to an agent. And you're prepared, in case they ask for a chapter outline. First, though, you need one more item to complete your proposal package—a cover letter.

Unlike the query letter, which goes out unaccompanied (except for the SASE) and often unsolicited, the cover letter is part of a solicited package and literally covers that package. Its job is to reintroduce you to the agents or editors who asked to see more and to remind them of what your project is.

Just as your query letter was designed to get your foot in the door, the cover letter and the package it covers strive to make sure you can keep it there—and walk inside.

No less important than your other selling tools, this letter must be professional, typo- and error-free and well written.

GREETINGS AND SALUTATIONS

With your query letter you might have floundered a second or two before settling on the correct, formal salutation. But now you've been provided a clue for your cover letter's greeting. If the request for more you received came in the form of a letter or E-mail, your clue comes in the way the agent or editor addressed you. If it's "Dear Blythe" or "Dear Marshall," you may follow in kind and address the editor or agent by first name. But if the letter came to "Dear Ms. Camenson" or "Dear Mr. Cook," you should continue to use the more formal address.

If the request for more came via telephone, take your cue from the tone of the conversation—chatty and relaxed or more formal and professional.

WHAT DO YOU SAY AFTER YOU SAY HELLO?

Find a balance in your cover letter between gushy chattiness ("Hiya, pal!") and formalistic language ("In re your communiqué of 1 November . . ."). Clear, conversational language works best: "I appreciate your willingness to review my proposal for *The Middle of Midnight*." Or, "As you requested, I've enclosed my manuscript. . . ."

Whatever you say now, say it clearly and concisely, brief and to the point.

Include these items as appropriate:

1. Reminder of Face-to-Face Meetings

Don't assume the editor or agent remembers that quick conversation you had during the second afternoon break at the writers conference. It may have been one of the most exciting encounters of your life, but unless you spilled coffee on his tie or wine on her blouse (and we *don't* recommend this), the meeting probably wasn't quite as memorable for the publishing pro.

Remind them they "know" you: "I enjoyed chatting with you at the Seymour WriterFest last week." Don't overdo the reminder, however. "I was enchanted by your amusing anecdotes" is laying it on way too thick, as is, "I found your comments on the state of literary publishing in America today to be both insightful and inspiring."

With this reminder of where you met, don't forget to mention that they requested your package. Solicited submissions usually gain quicker attention than unsolicited ones.

2. Summary of Past Communication

Just as you need to remind the agent or editor of a past meeting, you also must allude to past written correspondence. You can't assume editors or agents remember previous letters, no matter how enthusiastic they seemed at the time. They deal with hundreds of people.

The most important prior communication is an agent's or editor's stated willingness to read your proposal. Again, don't fail to remind them that your proposal is requested, not unsolicited.

3. Referral Reminder

If you have a referral, you pointed that out in your query letter. The cover letter provides a second chance to lay this important card on the table. "As I mentioned to you in my query letter, my friend Jacquelyn Mitchard, author of *The Deep End of the Ocean*, indicated you might be especially interested in my protagonist, James Lee Dickey."

4. Type and Length of Novel

Repeat the vital statistics you gave in your query letter—your novel's genre and word count. "*The Middle of Midnight* is a historical novel, approximately 80,000 words."

5. Pitch Line

That one-sentence summary, crafted with such sweat and care, serves you well here. Include it in your cover letter. *The Middle of Midnight* "depicts the hours leading up to the surrender of Gen. Robert E. Lee at Appomattox Court House, told from the point of view of the young soldier assigned to care for Lee's famous horse, Traveller."

6. Your Credentials

In your query letter you gave a full account of who you are and what qualifies you as the author of this book. You don't have to go into such detail here, but certainly remind them of the most pertinent parts, things such as relevant professional experience, related publishing credits and your time spent in the location in which your book is set.

WHEN YOU'RE READY TO STOP . . .

Stop! Don't repeat yourself. Don't beg. Don't state the obvious ("Enclosed please find my proposal, along with a self-addressed . . . "). They know what to do.

COVER LETTER FORMAT

Just as with the query, the cover letter is a business letter and should be formatted as such. Use letterhead stationery, a standard typeface and a quality printer. Make sure your letter is single-spaced with either indented paragraphs (with no line spaces between them) or the more tidy block style. (Review chapter three for more details on letter formatting.)

Take a look at the sample cover letter on p. 191. It is a solid, concise cover letter from a first-time novelist who knows no one in the publishing industry and has never published a scrap of fiction in his life. Note, however, that he stresses the positives—his knowledge of the Civil War, his extensive research, his job as a volunteer curator at a Civil War museum. By mentioning these facts, he has given his proposal a chance to succeed.

Notice the following cover letter elements:
- reference to previous correspondence (first and third paragraphs)
- succinct summary statement (second paragraph)
- the reason the author has approached this particular agent—displaying a knowledge of the agent's work (third paragraph)
- strong credentials statement stressing positives (fourth paragraph)
- crisp, businesslike closing—no nonsense and no begging.

January 1, 2000

William G. Beymer
1234 Palm Court
Chambersburg, PA 12345-6789
(123) 456-7890
beymer@email.com

John Smith
Smith Literary Agency
1313 Thirteenth St.
New York, NY 10011

Dear Mr. Smith,

I appreciate your willingness to review my proposal for *The Middle of Midnight*, a historical novel of approximately 80,000 words. Your response to my query letter of December 23, 1999, was most encouraging.

My novel depicts the hours leading up to the surrender of Gen. Robert E. Lee at Appomattox Court House, from the point of view of the young soldier assigned to care for Lee's famous horse, Traveller.

As you may remember, I queried you initially because you served as the agent for John Haband's recent historical, *A Tide in the Affairs of Man*. My book deals with a similar theme.

I was born and raised in Chambersburg, the only northern town burned by southern troops during the Civil War. My interest in that battle dates to my earliest memories. I've done extensive independent research, including reading unpublished correspondence from Civil War soldiers to their families and visiting all of the major battle sites.

Based on this research, I've published several articles on the subject in historical journals. I'd be glad to provide clips. I've been a volunteer curator at the Chambersburg Civil War Museum for six years.

I look forward to hearing from you.

Sincerely,

William G. Beymer

THREE WAYS TO REVEAL YOU'RE AN AMATEUR

Here are three bits of information you should *not* include in your cover letter:

1. notification of rights offered (e.g., "First North American Serial Rights")
2. Social Security number
3. response deadline ("Please respond within two weeks")

Why not?

I. Notification of Rights Offered

Your contract will cover all ancillary or subsidiary rights, including paperback and foreign-language editions and adaptions to another medium. (Yes, that means movie rights, among other things.) You or your agent will negotiate these matters when the publisher offers that contract. Including a rights notification in your cover letter indicates that you don't know what you're doing.

2. Social Security Number

Publishers need your Social Security number when they pay you money so they can report that payment to the Internal Revenue Service. Nobody's offering you any money yet.

3. Response Deadline

You probably wouldn't kick off a job interview by leaning back in the chair, plopping your feet on the interviewer's desk and saying, "I'll need to know your decision by this afternoon. I've got plans to make." You wouldn't if you really wanted to get the job, anyway. Establishing a response deadline for the agent or editor is pretty much the same thing—and every bit as well received.

Yes, it's hard to wait. And yes, some editors and agents take what seems to be an interminably long time to respond. In many cases, it seems interminable because it is interminable. But that doesn't give you license to be rude and presumptuous, and to do so would create a horrible impression.

THIRTY-EIGHT WAYS TO WRITE A ROTTEN COVER LETTER

How many of the thirty-eight mistakes in this cover letter do you recognize?

January 1, 2000
William Bonney, novelist ❶
1234 Backwoods Rd.
Vilanelle, LA 98765-4321

The Super Agent Go-Getter Agency
1313 Thirteenth Ave. SE
New York, NY 10011
©William Bonney, 1999 ❷, all rights reserved ❸

Dear Super, ❹

    I enjoyed the three hours I spent with you at the Pennsylvania Writers Conference. ❺ I wondered where you had disappeared to, but I decided to send you my manuscript anyway ❻ and give you the unprecedented opportunity ❼ to represent one of the finest fiction novels written in the twentieth century. ❽

continued on next page

---

1. If you have to tell them you're a novelist, you're already in trouble. Plus, it sounds pretentious.
2. A copyright statement is one of the three tip-offs that you don't know what you're doing. It also indicates you don't really trust the agent.
3. Yes, that's basically what *copyright* means. No need to say it once, much less twice.
4. That's "Mr. Agent" to you!
5. But we'll bet the agent didn't. Billy has abused the agent's willingness to spend time with writers.
6. Big mistake. The agent probably doesn't even want to see a proposal from Billy. He certainly won't want the entire manuscript. Nor will he read it.
7. Oh, if only it were unprecedented. But alas, agents see this sort of thing all too often.
8. As opposed to a nonfiction novel? Fictional history? All novels are, by definition, fiction.

The Middle of Midnight examines the life and times ❾ of Gen. American Civil War ❿, also known as The War Between the States, or, as the Rebs called it, The War of Northern Aggression. ⓫

What makes this gripping novel ⓬ completely unique ⓭ is the fact that its author, yours truly, ⓮ tells the tale from the point of view of the young soldier assigned to take care of Lee' famous horse, Traveler. ⓯ You may not get this right away, since everything takes place in the kid's head, but it comes clear after about the third chapter. ⓰ If Tom Clancy had decided to write about the Civil War, the result might have been *The Middle of Midnight.* ⓱

My writing teacher at Vilanelle Tech says the first chapter is the best thing she's seen all semester ⓲—and she doesn't hand out the compliments at the drop of a hat, ⓳ believe you me. ⓴ Several classmates told me they literally ㉑ could not put this book down. It's that good. ㉒

continued on next page

9. *Life and times* is a vague, empty cliché.
10. We'll just bet Mr. Agent already knew that . . .
11. . . . and had no desire or need to know the rest of it.
12. Silly brag and boast.
13. Is that like being "totally pregnant"? *Unique* is not subject to qualification.
14. Flippant, overly familiar tone.
15. We might put a little more faith in Billy's expertise if he had spelled the name of the horse correctly.
16. If you feel the need to explain the first two chapters, you don't stand a chance of selling them.
17. But probably not.
18. Now there's a real celebrity endorsement!
19. Or the drop of a cliché?
20. See (14).
21. No, they told him figuratively (unless Billy coated his manuscript with glue).
22. Inappropriate boast.

I haven't had anything published yet, **㉓** but that goes to show how rotten the publishing world is today, **㉔** when a real talented writer **㉕** can't get published, and all those hacks like Tom Clancy **㉖** keep cranking out all that garbage **㉗** and selling millions of copies. **㉘**

I've been a Civil War buff ever since I took an American history class last semester, **㉙** and I really know what I'm talking about. **㉚**

[The letter goes on in this manner for another sixteen pages. **㉛** We've skipped to the closing.]

I'm not going to grovel or anything, **㉜** but I'd really really really appreciate your taking me on. **㉝** It would mean a great deal to me, and also to my mother, who wants to prove to my old man that I really can amount to something after all. **㉞**

Let me know in the next couple of weeks. **㉟** If you're not smart enough to snap this surefire novel up, I'll bet somebody else will be! **㊱**

See you on the best-seller list, **㊲**

Billy the Kid **㊳**

23. A fact that will be painfully obvious to the agent by now. Stress the positive in your credentials statement.
24. The agent is, of course, an integral part of that "rotten" publishing world.
25. See (22).
26. Wasn't Tom Clancy a great paragon of writers a couple of paragraphs ago?
27. Like the sort of "garbage" the agent would very much love to represent.
28. Selling millions of copies is the idea!
29. With references like that, Billy doesn't need any detractors.
30. See (22).
31. Something a cover letter must never do! Keep it to under a page.
32. Billy *is* groveling, of course. Not very attractive, is it?
33. Is this an application for adoption?
34. A biographical detail the agent doesn't want or need to know.
35. Agents are busy people and don't appreciate having demands put on their time. They'll get back to you according to *their* schedule, not yours.
36. Don't bet the rent money.
37. Now that we wouldn't bet on!
38. Billy is presuming that he and the agent are good enough friends that he doesn't have to be professional, not that it matters at this point. He could have signed this "Clueless."

PART
THREE

THE RESULT

CHAPTER
EIGHT

HANDLING THE WAIT
—AND THE REJECTION

"If I like it, I like it. If I don't, I don't."   —John Scognamiglio, Zebra Books

H ere's our definitive word about waiting: Don't!
You've bundled up your proposal and sent it out into the world. You feel that mixture of fear and anticipation all writers experience at such times. You cringe at stories of manuscripts lost in the mail. Every trip to the mailbox becomes an experiment in approach-avoidance conflict. You want the letter to be there—and yet you're terrified that it will be.

How can you possibly bear the waiting?

By *not* just waiting for one single minute. Don't stare at the mailbox. Don't listen for the footfall of the postal carrier. Don't haunt the post office. And, especially, don't call the agent or editor to see if he's received your proposal. First, it will bug him. Second, you can easily dispel that anxiety by enclosing a self-addressed stamped postcard along with your material. And third, the U.S. Postal Service has a remarkably good record for reliability. The odds of your package getting lost are really quite small.

Instead of wasting your time waiting, get busy on your next novel. We won't advise you not to think about your proposal; that isn't possible. You wouldn't be human if you didn't care—passionately. But when you catch yourself thinking about it, gently send those thoughts away and get back to work. Waiting won't bring an answer one minute sooner, and worrying won't change that answer.

"A writer's job is writing," agent George Nicholson reminds us, "and the writer should continue to write, regardless of whether what he or she has written is currently selling."

HOW TO ANALYZE THE SILENCE

Having said that, we know you'll do some waiting and wondering anyway. We all do, especially the first few times out.

"They've had it for four weeks now," you think. "That's a good sign. They must be considering it."

Next, despair chases optimism.

"They've lost the manuscript," your inner voice wails. Or "It was so bad, they threw it out." Or even, "They haven't stopped laughing long enough to put the rejection slip in the envelope."

What does the silence mean—if it means anything at all? Does a longer wait mean you're in the running?

Maybe.

"How I approach my submissions is in the nature of triage," agent Nancy Yost says. "The ones that are going to die, you get rid of right away. The ones that you are really excited about, you ask for right away. The ones that look as if there might be something there but don't really stand out tend to sit the longest."

"We respond fairly quickly to the ones that clearly aren't right for us," says editor Kent Brown. "It is the same with the one or two we get a year that hit us over the head. The problem lies with all the ones that are in between. We try to figure out what to say to the authors to make it right."

So, yes, the easy rejection will probably come fast. If your project is under consideration, the response might be slower. But we'll stand by our original advice—all such speculation is futile. Get on with your work and let the agents and editors do theirs.

HOW LONG SHOULD YOU WAIT?

Please don't take anything we've said so far to indicate that we think you should sit quietly for weeks, months or forever while the editor or agent remains silent. If an agent or editor asked to see your proposal, you deserve an answer, and you shouldn't have to wait forever for that answer. (If, on the other hand, you disregarded our advice and sent out sample chapters or even the whole manuscript unsolicited, you might not hear back at all—especially if you also neglected to enclose an SASE. If that's the case, chalk it up to experience, start over with a new agent or editor, and do it the right way.)

How long is long enough to wait for a reply?

"I dislike it when an author calls up two weeks or a month after she sent in her project and wants to know if I read it yet," editor Karen Taylor Richman says.

Reviewing a proposal can take two or three months. Many agents send manuscripts through as many as four readers to get additional opinions.

Add extra time if you've approached a publisher directly rather than going through an agent. "I will read unagented manuscripts," editor Laura Anne Gilman says, "but my response time is longer, somewhere between three and five months, longer if something's getting a second reading, simply because of the sheer volume." Agented manuscripts get a faster response, Gilman says—another good argument for seeking an agent in the first place.

"I think it's a mistake for authors to wait three to six months to find out whether or not we ever got their manuscript," editor Kent Brown says. "The process of writing is slowed down too much by that. And we're doing our best not to get too far behind."

There's no set rule about waiting time. It varies with the publisher and the agency. It also varies depending on the editor's or agent's workload. Most professionals publish estimated response times with their guidelines or in the marketing guides. We suggest you take the maximum estimated response time and add a week. If the agent promises a response in "two to six weeks," take the six weeks, add the one-week cushion and plan on waiting seven weeks before following up. Then take out your calendar and mark the target follow-up date so you won't forget. (Believe it or not, if you get busy on new projects, you actually might!)

Patience is more than a virtue here. It's a necessity if you want to preserve your sanity and establish good working relationships with editors and agents. "Be patient," agent Frances Kuffel says. "The more patience a writer has with us, the more trust a writer has that we're not pulling strings, the better."

HOW TO FOLLOW UP

Some agents and editors won't respond to your query letter—not a phone call, not a letter, not even a form rejection slip. It's a cold, hard fact of publishing life. They are very busy people. Many are inundated with queries. They do their best to keep up, but sometimes the rejects go straight into the recycle bin—especially those that come without the SASE.

Don't worry about it. Don't analyze the silence. And don't bother following up on an unanswered query. You'll just be wasting your time and theirs. Move on. If you're marketing smartly—targeting your queries and sending to several likely editors or agents—you'll be too busy to worry about the no-shows.

A solicited manuscript is a different matter. Once an agent or editor has asked to see all or a portion of your novel, he owes you a response to your work. If you don't receive one, you have two follow-up options: a short note or a phone call.

There's something to be said for a written follow-up. A note won't intrude on the editor's or agent's workday, and thus it's less likely to seem pushy or annoying. Also, you can work out the wording carefully, just as you did with the original query, making sure you create a good impression.

Here is an example of an effective follow-up note—again, typed neatly on your letterhead stationery.

That's all you need. Keep it short and to the point, with a reminder that the manuscript was solicited and the date it was sent. And yes, even though the agent or editor already received an SASE from you

Dear [Agent's or Editor's Name],

I am writing to follow up on my manuscript, *The Middle of Midnight*, which I sent at your request three months ago, on January 2. Could you please let me know its status?

Sincerely,

with your original submission, send another one.

But a note is also easier to ignore, and a written exchange takes a lot longer than a phone call. And let's face it: The major reason to send a note instead of phoning is because it's so much easier on your nerves. It can be nerve wracking to pick up the phone and call.

We suggest that you do call, but only if you do it right. When you make your call, don't beg or badger. Have a plan. Be businesslike. "I sent my manuscript of a Civil War historical, *The Middle of Midnight*, on January 2. I'm wondering if there has been any decision on the project."

You might get a brush-off or an evasive nonanswer: "Ms. Agent is in conference right now. I'm sure you'll be hearing from us soon." (Translation: Don't call us, and we probably won't call you, but we will get to your manuscript eventually.)

You might get shot right between the eyes: "If you haven't heard from us, it means we're not interested."

But you might get confirmation they've received your material and an estimate of how much longer you'll need to wait before getting a response.

And you might even get a quick interview with the agent! Have your pitch line ready and be prepared to answer questions about your book. You just might be able to do you and your novel a lot of good.

HOW TO HANDLE REJECTION

When the answer does come, it might of course be no. Some of our most successful novelists have suffered numerous rejections. Betty Smith's classic *A Tree Grows in Brooklyn* was turned down 10 times. Grace Metalious's blockbuster, *Peyton Place*, received 14 rejections before finding a publisher. Irving Stone's *Lust for Life* endured 17 rejections, then went on to sell twenty-five million copies. Cult classic *Zen and the Art of Motorcycle Maintenance*, by Robert M. Pirsig, was rejected 121 times.

"When I hear that Louis L'Amour was rejected some 350 times before his first publication, I can only say, 'try a thousand rejections and see me in the morning,' " says Robert W. Walker, author of the highly successful Instinct series of thrillers.

"I have been rejected by every major and minor publisher two and three times over on more than thirty novels or various speculative proposals," Walker says. "I liken it to being turned down by every girl in school for the big dance. After running out of candidates, it becomes actually quite funny."

Funny?

"Yes, I have scoffed at rejection," Walker says, "and yes, I have laughed in the face of rejection. It takes that and the patience and tolerance of Job to deal with the god of New York City—the publishing giants."

David Kaufelt once got a letter from a famous agent that said, "Dear Mr. Kaufelt, I can't do a thing with this and neither can you." Kaufelt shrugged off this "advice" and became a successful mystery writer.

One of the biggest parts of writing is getting rejected.

"Be prepared for rejection," Rob Cohen says. "As agents, we get more rejections than any author could ever imagine getting. It just becomes part of the business you're in."

Don't take those rejections personally. It does not reflect on you. It does not mean you are a bad writer. It only means that a particular agent or editor decided he couldn't sell your book right now.

Read that last sentence again, slowly. If you're like most of us, you're going to take some convincing. A rejection doesn't mean that the universe hates you. It doesn't mean you'll never make it as a writer. It doesn't reflect on your worth or talent. You'll drive yourself crazy trying to find deeper meaning in the rejection.

Fiction is extremely subjective. Nobody knows that better than the people who write it, but we forget that when we send our work out for judgment.

No means no, no more and no less. It doesn't mean you should quit.

"Even if I send an encouraging rejection letter, asking to see the next project," editor John Scognamiglio says, "sometimes I never hear from the writer again." And that's a big mistake. Agents and editors don't offer encouragement unless they think you've got a chance. You should get another proposal out to them as soon as you can. "I know that writing is tough and takes discipline, but if someone wants to be a writer, he should find the time for his craft. Decide how badly you want it and don't give up."

"Publishing is a very hard business," agent Martha Millard says, "subject to a lot of ups and downs. Writers who really want to succeed should not get discouraged. They should follow their own inspiration and keep trying. If they get rejected by one agent, they should try another."

Nancy Yost cautions new writers not to worry about form rejection letters. Writers "get upset because no one gave them any feedback," she says, but "sometimes the very best thing next to a quick yes is a very quick no. A lot of times, it's just that the agent or editor knows right away it's something they're never going to be interested in. It's got nothing to do with the quality of the work. If I'm not the right person to handle it, it's better they know right away."

If you want advice, editor Anne Savarese says, "it's better to seek it out in a class or writers group. When you send your work to a publisher, it should be something you are satisfied with. You shouldn't be expecting feedback."

WHEN TO REVISE AND RESUBMIT

Sometimes a no comes with suggestions. When that happens, allow yourself to feel very encouraged. Any personal attention is a good sign. And when an editor or agent speaks, listen. School is in session.

"Generally, if people do get a long reply, it means the editor is interested in the book and thinks it can be improved," Anne Savarese says. "He'll usually say so up front. But whether to revise or not is up to the writer. There are no guarantees. If the editor does give a practical, concrete tip, it's good to pay attention to that."

"If I think someone has promise," John Scognamiglio says, "I'll suggest revisions on the current work, and then I'm happy to take a second look at it."

"If it's something I can help with, I'll write back," agent Rob Cohen says, "but it will have to be very close to being finished. I'm not going to do an editor's job."

"If I really love a book but it needs work before I could sell it, I'll suggest that the author revise the work," agent Richard Henshaw says. "I won't even suggest it if I'm not convinced that I'd take the book on if the author succeeds in making the changes that I've suggested."

Should you listen when pros like Savarese, Scognamiglio, Cohen and Henshaw talk? You bet. If you do, you'll find yourself a giant step closer to getting your novel published.

You may get conflicting criticism. One agent loves your plot but not your hero. The next really buys the hero but thinks your plot limps. A third likes both plot and hero but finds your writing uninspired. You're obviously not going to be able to please them all and shouldn't even try. But, if you get the same consistent comment, and if that comment makes sense to you, it's time to rewrite.

After that rewrite, can you send your novel back to the same agent who rejected it before? If the agent asked to see a rewrite, absolutely. You'd be a fool not to. Send it back with a cover letter reminding them of your previous correspondence and their suggestions.

What about the agent who gave you encouraging comments but didn't offer to read a rewrite? You can feel fairly safe resubmitting your manuscript. Your cover letter should thank the agent for suggestions and point out how you followed them.

If an agent offered no hope the first time around, you're probably wasting your time and postage sending back the revised manuscript.

You could certainly get away with submitting the same manuscript with a different title to a different editor within the same publishing house you approached before. "One of my perverse pleasures in life," agent Kathleen Anderson says, "is to sell books to houses that have rejected them."

We're not suggesting that you do anything to your novel you don't feel right about. It's your story and your writing career. You have to make the final call. But we are urging you to listen carefully, with an open mind, to suggestions from publishing professionals. They may be leading you out of rejection and into publication.

▲

CHAPTER
NINE

HOW TO WORK
WITH AGENTS AND EDITORS

"Take the money and run."   —Ernest Hemingway

S o far we've looked at three possible reactions to your novel proposal sent to agents:

A. no response

B. "no"

C. "maybe"

Now let's talk about how to handle the response you've been waiting to hear all along. Let's get to "yes"!

Veteran writers have a bit of cynical sounding advice for novelists
savoring their first taste of success: Don't quit the day job. Rejoice,
yes. An agent's faith in your work is a wonderful affirmation, and that
faith carries weight in the marketplace.

Congratulate yourself. You've beaten huge odds and taken a giant
step on the journey to publication. But don't think the job's done,
and don't assume that gaining representation by an agent ensures
publication.

WHAT TO EXPECT WHEN AN AGENT SAYS YES

Most agents interested in representing you will offer you a contract
right away. Many will defer creating such a contract until they actually
make a sale for you. And a few still work on the basis of a handshake

and/or a verbal agreement, waiting to add a clause covering their representation in any publishing contract they get for you.

If you aren't offered an agent/client contract right away, don't panic. There's a good reason for this seemingly lackadaisical way of doing business—and it can work in your favor. Suppose you start off as a romance writer and your agent sells a book or two for you. But then you decide to branch out into another genre or nonfiction. That's fine, as long as your agent also handles those categories. If he or she doesn't, then a strict agent/client contract could bind you to a relationship that suddenly has become stifling.

If the agent handles only one genre, but you've signed a contract making it difficult or even impossible for you to seek representation elsewhere on other kinds of projects, you might be in a bind—unless, of course, your agent simply agrees to release you from the contract.

Without a contract, most one-genre agents would be willing to refer you and your project to another agent and continue to handle any other work of yours that falls into their specialty areas.

Not all agents work with contracts. Some will discuss their terms with you verbally or in a letter of intent, then attach an addendum to the publisher's contract for any sales they might make on your behalf. This is a perfectly legitimate and common way of operating.

However, more and more agents use a standard contract, and more and more writers insist on signing it. As with all contracts, when they're designed correctly, they protect both parties.

WHAT YOUR AGENT/WRITER CONTRACT COVERS

Here are some terms to look for in your agent/writer contract.

1. Material to Be Represented

You might have only one book completed now, so you aren't concerned about limiting the work your agent might represent for you. But, if you're a published nonfiction writer with established relationships with publishing houses, for example, you don't want to give a percentage of your advances for those projects to an agent who had nothing to do with those book deals. The contract must specify what work(s) your agent will represent.

2. Commissions

Most agents take 15 percent for domestic sales and 20 percent for overseas and film rights. Your contract must state the agent's commission.

3. Expenses

Some agents charge for photocopying, faxes, long-distance telephone calls, messenger services and other legitimate expenses. Make sure you know in advance how much and when you'll be charged for these expenses. You may want to seek a cap on the amount you're willing to spend.

4. Accountability

Good agents will report all submissions they make on your behalf and all responses from publishers. They will consult with you before accepting or rejecting any offer. A good contract spells out these obligations.

5. Termination

Your contract should also spell out procedures for ending your agent/client relationship. Most contracts allow for either party to do so with reasonable notice, but they also call for the agent to receive commission for any deals she initiated before the termination of the contract.

When an agent agrees to represent your novel, she becomes a powerful ally—a savvy marketer with contacts, credibility and inside information. Agents are highly motivated to get you a contract, because they don't get paid until and unless they get you one. The larger the advance they get for you, the larger their initial payday, too.

WHAT YOU NEED TO DO FOR YOUR AGENT

You should expect honest effort and open communication from your agent. Your agent has the right to expect no less from you.

Tell your agent about any previous submissions you've made and rejections you've received on your novel. Share all correspondence. Your agent must create an effective marketing strategy for you. Withholding relevant information from the agent makes about as much sense as lying to your doctor.

This underscores another excellent reason to seek an agent for your novel before you approach publishers directly. If you've already been rejected by a publishing house, the agent can't now approach them with the same project. Had the agent made the proposal in the first place, the publisher might have accepted it.

WHAT YOU SHOULDN'T DO

Don't try to do the agent's job for him. Allow your agent to represent you. You're entitled to phone from time to time for progress reports or to discuss new projects, but if you call too often, you'll soon become a pest.

If you run across leads—the name of an editor, for example, who might be looking for a book such as yours—pass them on to your agent. But expecting auctions or making other unreasonable demands won't fly either.

You and your agent now have a working relationship you both hope will be productive and profitable. But your agent is your representative, not your therapist or your best friend. Remember to keep this new relationship in its proper perspective.

HOW AGENTS WORK

Agents often use a variety of approaches when trying to sell your work. Some make phone calls to editors and pitch your work first; some even do it in person.

Let's watch agent Anne Hawkins in action. First she draws up a marketing plan and discusses it with the author. Then she calls the editor or editors to make arrangements to pitch the book in person.

"I then send out the manuscript with my own letter pitching the book," she says. "The letter is quite important, especially if several editors wind up reading the book at the same house. Almost all books undergo several readings.

"That all-important letter to the editor is almost always less than one page. I very briefly summarize the book—usually in one paragraph," Hawkins says. "Then, I say what I believe is special about the book or the author's qualifications in the second paragraph. In the last paragraph I give a deadline for responses and also my thanks for the editor's time."

Hawkins takes a lot of time and care with these letters. "If a writer has sent me a good query letter," she says, "I sometimes can use parts of it for my own pitch letter, but not too often."

Hawkins, of course, hopes to start a bidding war among publishers.

"Auctions are a lovely thing! And lucrative," she says. "You [the agent] do need that first offer from an editor to get started. That's called the 'floor offer'. Then if other editors expressed interest in the book, you spend a lot of time on the telephone convincing them to up the ante. Almost any book put out for a simultaneous submission can be a candidate for an auction."

WHEN YOU HAVE TO FIRE YOUR AGENT

You work so hard to get an agent! Would you really ever want to throw one away?

You should never give up on yourself, but you may have to give up on your agent. Even an excellent agent representing a great novel might fail—and not all agents are excellent. You may find that you aren't being adequately represented. A bad agent may even do you more harm than good. When that happens, you have to support your novel, not your agent. Knowing when to fire your agent is the first step. Knowing how to do so politely and painlessly is the second. We have suggestions for you on both.

Seven Reasons for Cutting Your Agent Loose

1. YOU NEVER HEAR FROM YOUR AGENT. Unseasoned writers sometimes have unrealistic expectations about how often their agents should call or write. There are lots of good reasons why an agent might not return your call. But if you and your work aren't important to your agent, you need a new agent.

2. YOUR AGENT DOESN'T KNOW WHO YOU ARE. When you finally get her on the phone, you get the distinct feeling she's desperately trying to remember if you're the historical romance set in the Civil War South or the tale of the mob set in 1920s Chicago. If she's lost track of you, you should lose her.

3. YOU DON'T KNOW WHAT YOUR AGENT IS DOING. You should be in on your agent's marketing plans for your novel. You should know where your manuscript has gone and what responses it has gotten. You have the right to see all correspondence regarding your novel. If your agent won't tell you about these things, tell your agent good-bye.

4. YOUR AGENT DOESN'T SEEM TO KNOW WHAT HE'S DOING. Your agent submitted your gothic romance to House of Westerns. Even you knew better than that! He's just hoping to make a lucky sale. Tell him his luck has run out.

5. YOU'VE GOTTEN LOST IN THE SHUFFLE. Your agent's office looks like a recycling center. She can never find important letters, contracts or royalty statements, and editors aren't getting the information they need from her. Your agent needs a workshop on clutter management. You need another agent.

6. YOU'RE ANYTHING BUT "AGENT'S PET." Your agent gives other clients better treatment. He's pushing them for the top markets, and you're getting the leftovers. You and your work deserve better.

7. YOUR AGENT'S THE ONLY ONE WHO THINKS SHE'S AN AGENT.
Anyone can call herself an agent, print up letterhead stationery and business cards, and start submitting manuscripts to publishers. If those manuscripts end up on the slush pile along with unsolicited material from unpublished writers, the publishers have decided that she isn't really an agent at all. You should decide the same thing. Get a real agent.

You can't afford to settle for an agent who lacks the experience, the drive, the contacts and the commitment your novel must have to stand a chance of getting published by a major house. Don't settle for less, and don't stay with a bad agent. Move on. Here's how.

How to Fire Your Agent

First and foremost, if you have a written contract, follow its conditions for termination to the letter. Most agreements stipulate a specific term for the relationship (a year or eighteen months is fairly typical), but most also allow for termination of the relationship by either party with proper notification.

If you don't have a contract, write a brief business letter to your agent, including the following points:

1. Inform the agent you wish to stop being a client because you feel the relationship is no longer beneficial to you.
2. Ask the agent to stop making submissions of your work.
3. Stipulate that the agent will continue to represent you for 60 days on any submissions that are still active.
4. Ask for a complete history of anyone who has seen your material.
5. If you choose, you can also ask for the return of any manuscripts the agent has.
6. State that for work already published, the agent will continue to receive royalties on your behalf and forward statements and your share of the income to you within thirty days of receipt.

Don't feel guilty. Authors change agents. Agents reject authors. It's all part of the business.

But burning your bridges isn't. It's not kind, and it's not good business. End on a positive note. This sample termination letter illustrates how to do that.

SAMPLE LETTER OF TERMINATION

Dear Mr Smith,

In accordance with the terms of our contract, I am notifying you that I would like to terminate our agent/writer relationship. Although I appreciate your efforts on my behalf, it doesn't seem that we are producing any successes together.

Please don't make any more submissions for my novel, *Rocky Road*. I understand that it is still being considered by two publishing houses, and if a positive response should come back from one of them within sixty days, you, of course, would continue to represent that project.

It is not necessary to return any copies of my manuscript to me.

Above all else, I want to thank you for your encouragement. You helped validate me and my fiction-writing ability, and without that, I doubt I would have had the confidence to start my second novel. I wish you the best, and I do hope we stay in touch.

Sincerely,

STARTING THE HUNT AGAIN

You probably think you should cover your work submission needs before you move on. It's a scary thought being on your own again, unrepresented. But the hunt for a new agent shouldn't begin until after you've terminated your relationship with your current agent.

And, if you plan to go it solo, without an agent, you shouldn't begin submitting your work directly to publishers until your agent/writer relationship has been officially terminated.

TEN STEPS YOUR MANUSCRIPT TAKES TO BECOME A NOVEL

Getting an offer for your novel can and should be a part of the business, too.

Here's how it happens when all goes well:

1. You write a wonderful novel.
2. You study your markets and select a slate of likely agents to represent your novel.
3. You write queries to those agents.
4. An agent likes your query and asks to see a proposal (a synopsis and the first three chapters, let's suppose), which you, of course, send to him.
5. An agent loves your synopsis and sample chapters and asks to read the entire manuscript, which you load into a cannon and fire back immediately!
6. An agent offers to represent your novel and you sign a client/agent contract.

   Time to break out the champagne? Not yet. But you might want to get it on ice, just in case.
7. Your agent creates your marketing strategy and mails out copies of your novel with a cover letter to selected editors. Some agents make telephone contact with likely editors before submitting your manuscript through the mail.
8. An editor decides (often after sending your manuscript around to several other readers for their opinion) that your novel has merit and might make a good addition to their list.

   Still not quite time for the celebration.
9. Unless she works for a very small house, the editor must now sell your book to her editorial board.
10. The editorial board has to convince the P&L (that's profit and loss) folks that the project makes economic sense.

    If all that adds up, the book contract comes next.

WHAT TO DO WHEN THE CONTRACT COMES

If your agent gets your book contract for you, he or she will also negotiate its terms on your behalf. If you sent your proposal directly to a publisher and got a contract for it, you might decide to negotiate the contract yourself.

Wherever that contract comes from, don't just sign it and send it back. Make sure you understand what you're signing.

Oh, you'll *want* to sign immediately—before they change their minds! Don't do it. Believe it or not, a bad contract can be a lot worse than no contract at all.

Read your contract carefully and then get some help. Call your agent or publisher for clarification of any points that aren't clear to you. Seek advice from published writers.

If you are agentless, you might want to pay an attorney to evaluate the contract—but only an attorney who knows literary property law. You might even want to seek representation by an agent at this point, even though you've successfully sold your book yourself. An agent can negotiate your contract for you and also guide future submissions. They're usually well worth their 15 percent.

Certain provisions of your contract may look horrible but turn out to be standard and no reason for alarm. The "hold blameless" clause, wherein the publisher disavows all knowledge of you if you get sued for libel, is especially scary.

Other inclusions may look harmless to you but may in fact cost you lots of money and limit your ability to market your work later. Phrases like "all rights" and "work for hire" are especially noxious.

Whether you receive a simple two-page contract or a twenty-two-page single-spaced cloud of legal vapor, be sure you understand it fully before you sign it. Don't be afraid to ask for changes. If an agent got you your contract, she'll continue to earn her commission now, negotiating on your behalf.

HOW YOU GET PAID

As the author, you get a royalty: a percentage of the price of every book sold. Publishers usually pay royalties on the full retail price of the book, but some pay on the net price, which could be half or less of the cover price.

Many publishers use a three-tiered royalty scale based on the number of books sold. For a first pressrun of fifteen thousand hardcover copies of your novel, for example, your royalty schedule might look like this:

> copies 1 to 5,000: 10 percent
>
> copies 5,001 to 10,000: 12.5 percent
>
> copies 10,001 and up: 15 percent

The contract may also call for different royalty percentages for books sold through book clubs or other special cases.

The publisher monitors sales and issues a royalty statement and a check for royalties due you—usually quarterly, but in some cases twice a year or even just annually. These royalty statements may be quite tricky to read (unless your day job involves spreadsheets and double entry bookkeeping). If you have an agent, ask him or her to explain the data for you. The agent may have to call the publisher for clarification. If you don't have an agent, call the publisher directly with your questions.

What about that seventeen million dollars Stephen King got just for signing his contract?

That's an advance. Although many small publishers will not offer you an advance, all large publishers and most midsized ones will. But your advance will have considerably fewer zeros to the left of the decimal point than Stephen King's.

Whatever the size of the advance, you need to know it by its full name: advance against royalties.

If you fulfill the terms of your contract and submit an acceptable manuscript, the advance is yours to keep, even if your book goes directly to remainder table oblivion. But you don't get another penny until your book earns back its advance.

Let's do the math, using the royalty schedule above. Suppose you received a $20,000 advance, and your book sells for $20. For the first 5,000 sales, you earn $2 per book, or $10,000. But instead of a check in the mail, you get a royalty statement indicating your balance as "($10,000)," or negative $10,000, meaning you still have to pile up another $10,000 to equal your advance before you begin earning more money.

How many more books do you have to sell before you that happens? (We'll wait while you get a pencil.)

The next 5,000 sales earn you 12.5 percent, or $2.50 per book. So the next 4,000 sales will earn back the second $10,000.

When copy number 9,001 sells (the first 5,000 at 10 percent, the second 4,001 at 12.5 percent), you break into positive royalty territory.

What about the paperback?

Generally, permission to issue your novel as a paperback constitutes a separate right with a separate advance and a separate royalty schedule. The same goes for the right to make a screenplay from your novel, the right to translate it into another language and the right to print up T-shirts with your protagonist's face on them. Agents earn their keep negotiating these ancillary rights for you.

OH YES, YOU WILL NEED EDITING

Once the contract is signed, you can sit back, put your feet up and wait for the royalties to pour in, right? Not even close.

Now your manuscript undergoes editing. The bigger the house, the more editors it will go through. You should be an active partner in the editing process. A writer has to have stamina and perseverance, even after a book has been accepted by an agent and an editor.

The editor doesn't really want to slice and dice your manuscript to the point where you barely recognize it. It just seems that way sometimes. Most editors subscribe to the same motto that guides doctors:

"First, do no harm." They want to preserve your voice in the novel while doing the necessary cleanup and clarification.

Your job will be to work with your editor, listening carefully to criticism and recognizing the value of her experience, perspective and insight. Pick your fights and defend your positions with reason, not emotion.

You may end up experiencing "irreconcilable differences" with your editor. It doesn't happen often, but it does happen. If you can't agree on revisions, the publisher retains the option of not publishing your book. In that case, they may even ask you to return all or part of your advance. Now you really need an agent/advocate to fight for you so you don't have to return the advance until and unless you sell your book to another publisher. If you don't have an agent, seek help from one of the writers groups listed in the appendix at the back of this book.

But such horrors are the rare exception. A willing author and a capable editor usually form a powerful team. Together, you can produce a better novel than you thought possible.

AFTER YOUR NOVEL'S PUBLISHED: A NEW JOB BEGINS

"The real work begins once you've sold a book and begin promoting it," agent Julie Castiglia says.

As a first-time author, you may be disappointed that you aren't immediately booked on *Oprah*. Publishers spend most of their promotional dollars on established authors (thus making them even more established).

But you can do a lot to help promote your book yourself, editor Kent Carroll says, and "the more attention a book gets, the better it sells."

The smaller the publisher, the more of the promotional load you'll have to shoulder. But even if HarperCollins or Bantam Books publishes your novel, you should do everything you can to get that book noticed. Along with your publishing contract, your publisher will send you a questionnaire asking, among other things, who should get review copies and where the publisher should seek personal appearances for you.

Give these questions time, effort and creative thought. Guide the marketing department to local talk shows. Give them names of specific book reviewers and editors of relevant specialty magazines and newsletters. Suggest stores where your novel might be the only book on the counter. Then be willing to put your body where your books are. To promote *The Year of the Buffalo*, Marshall has signed books in bookstores, of course, and has also sat behind a card table on Main Street, downwind from the hot dog stand, while a parade rolled by. Because the book has a minor league baseball motif, Marshall has shown up at ballparks—books in hand, smile on face. And he keeps a box of books in the trunk of his car. You just never know when you might run into somebody who wants to buy your book. It's all part of being an active promotional partner.

But bugging your publisher every day isn't!

"I think some writers read in a magazine somewhere that if you pester your publisher enough, they will do all of these things for you," Kent Carroll says. "Not true. If you pester your publisher enough, they may stop doing anything for you."

Don't bug them, but help them every way you can. You both want the same thing, after all—to sell as many copies of your book as possible.

HOW TO NOT BE A ONE-BOOK WONDER

Getting your first novel published will provide a sense of satisfaction like no other in the writer's world.

But you don't want your career as a novelist to end there—and neither does your agent.

The sad truth is, most first novels don't sell well. Agents and editors know this better than anybody. They're more likely to be interested in you if they believe you have more than one good book in you—possibly even a series based on the protagonist of your first novel.

When your second and third novels gain a growing and devoted audience, a publisher may even reissue that neglected first novel in a fancy new cover to a brand new readership.

The basic question is, of course, whether your book sold at least as well as your publisher anticipated (as evidenced by the size of your advance and the initial pressrun). But other factors may testify in favor of giving you a second outing, including strong reviews in important places.

Your job in all of this? Get into it for the long haul by developing story ideas, pitching the best of them to your agent or publisher and being willing to modify your story to the marketplace if necessary.

These sound like nice problems to have, don't they? Working with agents and editors might not always be fun, and sitting behind a pile of your own books in a bookstore waiting for somebody to pay attention to you can be embarrassing, but these are problems that come with publication, and that's what this book is all about.

WHEN YOU AREN'T GETTING TO YES

All of this is well and good for when you get that initial yes. But what should you do if you are only getting rejection after rejection? Should you give up? In a word, no.

"If you have a book you really believe in, and you really worked hard on it and think it's something good, you shouldn't give up," urges editor Anne Savarese. "There is a market for first novels out there, and though it is competitive, it's not impossible to get published. If writing is something you are committed to, you should keep trying and do everything you can to hone your craft."

"Rejection is something you have to get used to if you are going to be a writer," editor Jennifer Brehl says. "Only if you continue to write will you become a better writer. As a new writer, realize that it takes time to develop your work."

Send your work to other agents. Get started on a new project. Rewrite your book, taking helpful advice, while letting unhelpful criticism go.

"I admire people who continue to send me things, but only if their work has improved and only if they listen to advice—and only if they are appreciative and pleasant," agent Julie Castiglia says.

There's only one certainty in the publishing world: Your novel will never sell while it's sitting in your desk drawer.

"This manuscript of yours that has just come back from another editor—don't consider it rejected," best-selling novelist Barbara Kingsolver says. "Consider that you've addressed it 'To the Editor Who Can Appreciate My Work' and it has simply come back stamped 'Not at this address.' Just keep looking for the right address."

Apply the techniques you've studied in this book. Be patient and persistent. Believe in yourself and your work—and you will find the right address.

APPENDIX

RESOURCES FOR WRITERS

Although writing might seem like a lonely profession, smart writers take advantage of all the resources and support available to them. In this appendix we provide you with information on valuable reference books, newsletters and other publications geared toward writers, along with writers associations and on-line resources.

BOOKS AND TRADE PUBLICATIONS

Writer's Digest books can be ordered on-line at a discount through www.writersdigest.com or by calling F&W Publications at (800) 289-0963. Other books may be ordered on-line at amazon.com (www.amazon.com) or through any bookstore.

Helpful Reference Books

There are hundreds of good books out there. Here are some of the most helpful. We've starred the four you shouldn't miss.

***Guide to Literary Agents** (annual), Writer's Digest Books, 1507 Dana Avenue, Cincinnati, OH 45207.

We suggest you put your efforts toward finding an agent for your novel—and let the agent deal with the publishers. The guide lists five hundred agents and is divided into sections by those who charge fees and those who don't. (It's those who *don't* charge fees you want to approach. Make sure that the agent is a member of the AAR.) Each year the guide also includes helpful articles on topics such as writers conferences and query-letter writing.

Caution: With this and other marketing directories, you need access to the current year's edition. Things change fast in the publishing world.

Writer's Guide to Book Editors, Publishers, and Literary Agents, Jeff Herman, Prima Publishing, P.O. Box 1260, Rocklin, CA 95677-1260.

An agent himself, Herman describes the functions of editors, publishers and agents and helps you find your way in the publishing industry.

******The International Directory of Little Magazines and Small Presses***, Dustbooks, P.O. Box 100, Paradise, CA 95967.

As *Writer's Market* is to the large and midsized commercial publishers, this directory is to smaller, regional and independent presses. This reference is more than useful; it's an education in publishing.

Literary Market Place (LMP), R.R. Bowker Company, 121 Chanlon Road, New Providence, NJ 07974.

An industry standard, the yearly LMP lists the top 2,200 or so book publishers that meet Bowker's standards.

******Novel & Short Story Writer's Market***, Writer's Digest Books, 1507 Dana Avenue, Cincinnati, OH 45207.

With hundreds of pages of periodical and book publishers, this annual reference is a tremendous help for every writer who wants to publish a novel. Listings include current needs and taboos and specific tips from the publishers. This single volume can serve as your starting point in the search for a publisher.

The Writer's Handbook (annual), The Writer, 120 Boylston Street, Boston, MA 02116-4615.

This volume carries more articles but fewer listings than its better-known competitor, *Writer's Market.*

****Writer's Market*, Writer's Digest Books, 1507 Dana Avenue, Cincinnati, OH 45207.

With hundreds of pages of periodical and book publishers, this annual reference is a necessity for every writer who wants to publish. Listings include current needs and taboos and specific tips from the publishers. This single volume can serve as your starting point in the search for a publisher. Caution: With this and other marketing directories, you need access to the current year's edition. Things change fast in the publishing world.

Trade Publications

Creativity Connection. Marshall J. Cook edits this quarterly, sixteen-page newsletter for writers and small press publishers. You'll find how-to articles; profiles; market updates; reviews of newsletters, magazines and books; and a scam alert; along with contributions from several regular columnists. Contact Creativity Connection, 610 Langdon Street #622, Madison, WI 53703; phone (608) 262-4911; fax (608) 265-2475; E-mail: marshall.cook@ccmail.adp.wisc.edu.

(You can contact Marshall for any other reason through these addresses, too.)

Fiction Writer's Guideline. This is a bimonthly, eight-page newsletter, free to members of Fiction Writer's Connection, also available by subscription. Issues include the following columns: agent and editor interviews, author interviews, writing tips, how-to articles, conferences listings, markets, contests, Internet resources, "stormy weather" (scam) announcements and more. Coauthor Blythe Camenson is its editor and the director of Fiction Writer's Connection, as well. *Fiction Writer's Guideline* also accepts freelance submissions. Contact FWC, P.O. Box 72300, Albuquerque, NM 87195; (800) 248-2758; E-mail: bcamenson@aol.com; visit FWC's Web site at www.fictionwriters.com.

Obviously, we don't have a corner on the market. Here are some other fine resources.

ByLine. This excellent monthly magazine, established in 1981, offers instruction through feature articles and regular columns. They also publish freelance work and run numerous contests for writers in all genres. Editor Marcia Preston publishes one of the most positive and helpful writer resources around. Contact ByLine, P.O. Box 130596, Edmond, OK 73013.

Gila Queen's Guide to Markets. This is the best monthly marketing magazine we've encountered. Editor and "queen" Kathryn Ptacek publishes general marketing info, and each issue contains a thematic section on a particular genre (romance, sci-fi/fantasy/horror, children's/young adult, etc.) Contact Gila Queen, P.O. Box 97, Newton, NJ 07860-0097; (201)579-1537; E-mail: gilaqueen@aol.com; Web site: http://members.xoom.com/gilaqueen/gila.htm.

Poets & Writers Magazine. Excellent writer interviews and tons of information on writing contests, grants, awards and conferences make this thick, meaty bimonthly a fine resource for literature lovers. Contact 72 Spring Street, New York, NY 10012; phone (212) 226-3586; fax (212) 226-3963.

Small Press Review. Len Fulton's fine monthly supplements *The International Directory of Little Magazines and Small Presses* This title offers reviews and updates on small and independent publishers. Contact: Dustbooks, P.O. Box 100, Paradise, CA 95967; phone (916) 877-6110; fax (916) 877-0222; E-mail: dustbooks@telis.org.

Writer's Digest. The biggest and best known of them all, *Writer's Digest* magazine offers market updates, how-to articles and profiles of successful writers. The magazine is part of F&W Publications, which publishes books under five imprints (including Writer's Digest

Books), and runs its own book club for writers. Contact Writer's Digest, 1507 Dana Avenue, Cincinnati, OH 45207; (800) 289-0963.

Writer's News. A friendly, chatty monthly market update, mixing market updates, writing tips and quotes. The personality of its editor, Elizabeth Klungness, comes through on every page. Contact Tower Enterprises, 2130 Sunset Drive #47, Vista, CA 92083-4516; (760) 941-9293.

WRITERS ASSOCIATIONS
American Society of Journalists and Authors (ASJA)
1501 Broadway, Suite 302, New York, NY 10036 (212) 997-0947
E-mail: asja@compuserve.com; Web site: www.asja.org

The ASJA is leading the fight to protect writers' rights on-line. They supply information free via E-mail and maintain a Web site with updated information.

Fiction Writer's Connection
P.O. Box 4065, Deerfield Beach, FL 33442 (800) 248-2758
E-mail: bcamenson@aol.com; Web site: www.fictionwriters.com

FWC offers courses on writing and getting published, public and private message boards and chats for networking, tip sheets, interviews with editors and agents, a bookstore with Writer's Digest books available at a discount, reference links, two newsletters and a wealth of information for writers wanting to hone their craft and get published.

Horror Writers Association (HWA) site (http://www.horror.org/index.htp) states that HWA "was formed to bring writers and others with a professional interest in horror together, and to foster a greater appreciation of dark fiction in general."

Inkspot (http://www.inkspot.com) allows networking with other writers to share information. The message board is organized according to genre. The site also contains information on agents, markets, resource link, contests and conferences.

Mystery Writers of America, Inc.

17 E. Forty-Seventh St., 6th Floor, New York, NY 10017 (212) 888-8171

The leading national organization for mystery writers.

National Writers Club

1450 S. Havana, Suite 424, Aurora, CO 80012 (303) 751-7844

Writers don't have a union (and probably never will), but the National Writers Club is about as close as we come. With the ASJA, they're helping writers fight to protect their work and earn fair return for their labors.

The Pure Fiction site (http://www.purefiction.com/) states it's "packed with hundreds of links, book reviews and previews, and the sort of information you'll require, if you want to become a successful published author."

Romance Writers of America

3707 FM 1960 West, Suite 555, Houston, TX 77068 phone: (281) 440-6885 fax: (281) 440-7510 Web site: http://rwanational.com

The group for romance writers, with active state chapters.

Science Fiction and Fantasy Writers of America, Inc.

5 Winding Brook Dr., Suite 1B, Guilderland, NY 12084

Another good bet for the genre writer.

Short Mystery Fiction Society (http://www.thewindjammer.com/ smfs/index_low_bandwidth.html) caters to writers and readers of short mysteries. According to their Web site, "Good things come in small packages—especially mysteries."

The **Writers Guild of America** site (http://www.wga.org/) offers information about the Guild itself, author interviews, a message board, research links and articles.

ON-LINE RESOURCES

In the last few years the Internet and World Wide Web have grown tremendously, with an estimated sixty million users taking advantage of all it has to offer. Among that huge figure are writers, those seeking guidance and those offering it.

What does the Internet have to offer writers? In the following pages we highlight general sites for writers, as well as bookstores, publishers, agents, on-line courses, writers associations, on-line newsletters, sites that announce conferences and contests, research sites, even sites where you can find help brushing up on your grammar.

General Sites for Writers

writersdigest.com (www.writersdigest.com). This site features market updates, publishers' guidelines, a weekly E-mail newsletter, "Market of the Day" and much more, all from the same people who bring you *Writer's Digest* and *Fiction Writer* magazines and *Writer's Market*.

Publishers

Most major publishers and many small presses now have Web sites where you can order books, view on-line catalogs and get an idea of the type of books each publishes. On-line browsing provides an easy way to target potential markets for your projects. Fire up your Web browser and enter keywords, such as *book publishers*, or specific publishing companies, such as Random House or Contemporary Books. Some sites have obvious Web addresses (e.g., www.harpercollins.com); others you'll have to search for.

Agents

As you've learned in previous chapters, agents don't generally advertise for clients, whether in print or on the Net. Having said that, some very respectable agents have Web pages and are listed in various places on the Net. Be careful before submitting any work to agents you find on the Net. Just as in "real life," make sure agents you find on-line are AAR members and agree to adhere to a code of professional ethics. You could get lucky—or you could walk into a scam.

With that caveat out of the way, here are some sites for agents on the Internet.

Authorlink! Literary Agency Directory (http://www.authorlink .com/agents.html) has a listing of agents and provides tips on what each agent handles, how to query them, any recent sales and the number of clients.

The Internet Directory of Literary Agents (http://www.writers.net /agents.html) allows only non-fee-charging agents to be listed at the site. However, they can't police every listing that comes to them.

You can search for specific agents or browse through listings by name, agency, state and specialization. Some very reputable agencies are listed there, including Donald Maass Literary Agency and Elaine Davie Literary Agency.

Literary Agents: A Guide for Poets and Fiction Writers (http:// www.pw.org/info3.htm) is sponsored by Poets & Writers, Inc. The site has information about agents and a listing of reference books to help you find agents.

WordSmith's WebBook (http://alfalfapress.com/) contains a listing of agents on the Web, including information on fee-charging agents. Information also includes how to query by E-mail. No endorsement is implied by an agent being listed on their pages.

On-Line Courses

Taking a class on-line offers tremendous benefits. Tuition fees are usually very reasonable, you don't have to fight traffic or hunt for a parking space, and you can come to class in your pj's. Programs consist of a combination of on-line class time, E-mail consultations and lessons, and library files for you to download and study at your leisure.

America Online's Online Campus (keyword: Campus) has the most comprehensive course offerings. Departments range from business and computer studies to hobbies, languages and, of course, writing.

AOL's writing department includes courses on every aspect of writing and getting published, including Blythe's "How to Approach Editors and Agents," "How to Write Winning Query Letters" and "How to Write a Novel Synopsis." Other courses cover the different genres—mystery, romance, sci-fi, etc.—creative writing and also non-fiction topics such as travel, magazine or grant and proposal writing. Course fees range from twenty-five dollars to fifty dollars.

For non-AOL members, the Web has a variety of classes, including university extension programs (such as from the University of California) and writing-related courses offered at specific sites belonging to different writers associations. Do a keyword search with the name of the university in which you are interested or contact the different writers associations listed earlier in this appendix.

Here are four sites to get you started.

SFNovelist Writing Workshop (www.sfnovelist.com/index.html) is a site for those interested in writing hard science sci-fi novels. They offer a moderated on-line writing group with a number of published authors, physics professors and technical people, as well as an E-mail discussion group.

Vostock's Facts (http://www.vostocksfacts.com/) is intended as a complete resource of current information and data on scientific criminal investigation. It is designed for writers as well as law enforcement professionals. They also offer on-line courses for writers.

Writers on the Net (http://www.writers.com/) offers classes, tutoring and mentoring and writers groups. Writers on the Net is a group of published writers who are also experienced teachers. There are services here of use to poets, business writers, fiction writers, journalists, essayists, mystery writers, science fiction and fantasy writers, playwrights and screenwriters, horror writers, writers of historical fiction, academic writers and those who simply have a passion for writing and would like to write better.

Writers' Village University (http://www.communitech.net /~t-zero/) offers a free on-line interactive course for fiction writers and students. To register or learn more about Writers' Village visit their Web site.

On-Line Newsletters

The Electronic Newsstand, Inc.'s enews.com (http://www.enews .com/) allows you to find almost any magazine you're looking for. A new feature lets you customize your own newsstand by selecting from lists of specific magazine categories, rather than having to sift through the thousands available on the database.

MediaFinder (http://www.mediafinder.com/) is a searchable database of newsletters, magazines, catalogs and journals.

Tidbits (http://www.fictionwriters.com) is a free on-line newsletter put out by FWC director Blythe Camenson. It lists events, member success stories and scams to watch out for. Also available by E-mail at bcamenson@aol.com.

Writer's Digest (www.writersdigest.com) offers an E-mail newsletter with author interviews, market news, subscriber-only articles and other information for writers. Subscribe through their Web site.

Writers Conference Sites

The Guide to Writers Conferences, by ShawGuides (http://www
.shawguides.com/cgibin/rbox/sg.pl?s=0) is an on-line source for more
than four hundred conferences, workshops, seminars and festivals.
Their Web site is frequently updated, and you can access the guide
for free. You can search according to city, state, keyword or conference
name.

Romance Writers of America (http://rwanational.com/) hosts one
of the largest annual writers conferences in the U.S. Their Web site
also includes information on state RWA chapters, which often organize their own conferences.

Screenwriters Online (http://www.screenwriter.com/writerscalendar
.html) lists conferences by state. It also includes Canadian and international listings.

Writing—Conferences & Workshops (http://www.hukilau.com
/yellowpage/db/workshops.shtml) provides links to writers conference information all over the Internet.

Writers Write (http://www.writerswrite.com/conf.htm) lists conferences with enough information for you to decide if the conference is
right for you. The site includes addresses, phone numbers and E-mail
addresses for requesting additional information.

Yahoo! (http://msn.yahoo.com/social_science/communications
/writing/conferences/) has a listing of annual writers conferences, such
as the Maui Writers Conference or the Indiana University Writers'
Conference.

The Zuzu's Petals Literary Resource: Regional Writers' Resources
(http://www.zuzu.com/worklink.htm) offers an alphabetical listing of
conferences and workshops with links to each site.

Contest Listings

ClueLass Opportunities for Mystery Writers (http://www.cluelass .com/) has a listing of contests of interest to mystery writers.

Inkspot (http://www.inkspot.com/bt/market/contests.html) announces writing contests in a variety of genres and categories.

The Literary Times (http://www.tlt.com/news/wrkshp.htm) lists upcoming contests and features an article on entering competitions.

Loft Contests and Grants (http://www.loft.org/loft/contests.htm) sponsors both poetry and fiction-writing contests. At the site you'll also find the article "The Guideline Blues: Tips on How to Enter Contests."

MovieBytes Contest List (http://www.moviebytes.com/mb_contests .cfm) lists screenwriting contests.

The Romance Club (http://www.theromanceclub.com/writers/trcco nte.htm) sponsors a contest for book-length romance manuscripts four times a year.

The Market List (http://www.marketlist.com/) caters to writers of science fiction, fantasy and horror. You can download The Market List for information on anthologies, contests and markets or view the contest listings on-line.

Word Museum (http://www.wordmuseum.com/) sponsors writers' competitions in several categories, including romance, mainstream, science fiction and children's. At this site you can opt to enter your writing or act as a judge.

Research Sites

Encyberpedia (http://www.encyberpedia.com/ency.htm) lists such subjects as medicine, sports, biographies, fact books, legal and government.

Internet Research (http://www.purefiction.com/pages/res1.htm) is a detailed site for Internet research with step-by-step instructions on how to find what you're looking for.

The Internet Sleuth site (http://www.isleuth.com/) offers specialized search engines for a variety of topics, including reference, government or news. If you don't find what you need with one search engine, you can try another one until you do.

MapBlast (http://www.mapblast.com) will produce a detailed map within moments of your recording the address and zip code. Perfect to make your novel settings accurate. They claim to have data on every street in North America.

John McDonnell's Researcher's Toolkit (http://www.geocities .com/wallstreet/6100) contains different categories to help narrow your search, then it offers the best links for that particular subject. There's also an "expert" category, listing two hundred Web sites where you can find experts to answer your questions.

The Noble Group Internet Directories (http://www.experts.com/) gives you access to thousands of listings that contain information about experts, spokespersons and consultants in all fields.

Ready Reference Using the Internet (http://k12.oit.umass.edu/rref .html) provides information on just about any topic, from adoption to digestive disorders to Social Security.

Research-It! (http://www.itools.com/research-it/research-it.html) is a reference desk that offers search facilities for just about anything. It features language translations, Bible references, maps, facts and much more.

StudyWeb (http://www.studyweb.com/) lists more than fifteen thousand quality research links, in categories such as health and medical, history and culture, geography, and business.

Wired Cybrarian (http://www.wired.com/cybrarian/) is *Wired* magazine's guide to research on the Net. You'll find information on companies, people, breaking news, government data, Web page design specs, images, scientific research, books, games and stock prices.

Writers Free Reference Desk (http://www.writers-free-reference .com/) provides copyright information, quotations, links to newspapers, maps, ancient literature and links to Internet libraries.

My Virtual Reference Desk (http://www.refdesk.com/) is Marshall's favorite starting point for researching any question. Also check out a comprehensive on-line library at http://www.elibrary.com/.

NewsLink (http://www.newslink.org/news.html). Need current events information on a specific town or city? Wouldn't it be great to have access to the local newspaper? You do—thousands of dailies, weeklies and specialty papers are on-line and available to you through AJR NewsLink.

Grammar Sites
The Basic Prose Style and Mechanics page (http://www.rpi.edu /web/writingcenter/text/proseman.html) has different sections for prose style and punctuation and mechanics.

Superteach Free Services for Students (http://nz.com/webnz/check ers/free2.html) will help improve your proofreading skills, grammar and your knowledge of slang.

The Elements of Style, by William Strunk Jr., is on-line (http:// www.columbia.edu/acis/bartleby/strunk/). This reference book has the basic rules of usage and includes principles of composition with examples. You'll also find commonly misused or misspelled words and expressions.

Grammar and Style Notes, by Jack Lynch (http://andromeda.rutgers .edu/~jlynch/writing/) is another grammar and style reference book available on-line.

The **Grammar Grabbers** site (http://www.interlog.com/~bcutler /home.html) takes what is for some a difficult subject and has fun with it. Home page categories include, "Noooo! Don't Use THAT Word!" and " 'Grammar' Moses."

Grammar Queen (http://www.grammarqueen.com) allows you to pose your grammar question on-line and get answers from experts.

Mistakes in Writing (http://www.sff.net/people/roger.allen/mistakes .htm) showcases *The Standard Deviations of Writing* by Roger Mac-Bride Allen. Common errors are addressed in detail.

On-line English Grammar (http://www.edunet.com/english/gram mar/index.html) offers language practice pages and help.

Resources for Writers (http://www.execpc.com/~dboals/write.html) has around two hundred links to writers sites, some of which are related to grammar.

Miscellaneous

Writing a book set in the South, in a borough of New York or a section of Boston? You'll want to make sure your characters' speech reflects their locale. At the **American Slanguages** site (http://www .slanguage.com) you can choose from several U.S. cities and foreign countries and learn how the locals talk.

And just for fun, check out The Word Detective (http://www.users .interport.net/~words1/index.html).

ABOUT THE AUTHORS

Blythe Camenson

Blythe Camenson is a full-time writer with forty books and numerous articles to her credit. She is the director of Fiction Writer's Connection (FWC), a membership organization for new writers, and has been an instructor in AOL's Online Campus since 1995, teaching "How to Approach Editors and Agents," "How to Write Winning Query Letters" and "How to Write a Novel Synopsis." Through these courses and FWC she has helped to answer the questions of hundreds of new writers.

Blythe Camenson has published dozens of nonfiction books with NTC Publishing/Contemporary Books, Chicago. She is also the author of *Working in the Persian Gulf: Survival Secrets for Men and Women* (Desert Diamond Books, 1991, 1993).

Her articles and photographs have appeared in numerous publications. Her three novels, *Broken Connections, Widow* and *Parker's Angel*, are in the hands of her literary agent. The first two had movie options with major production companies.

Marshall J. Cook

Marshall J. Cook teaches workshops, seminars and credit courses on writing and editing, creativity, stress management, and media relations for the University of Wisconsin-Madison, Division of Continuing Studies, where he is a professor in the arts. He's a frequent speaker at conferences nationwide and edits Creativity Connection, a national newsletter for writers and independent publishers.

His novel, *The Year of the Buffalo*, was published by Savage Press in April 1997. He is also the author of nine nonfiction books and has appeared on *The Oprah Winfrey Show* as a guest expert on time management.

Marshall is a frequent contributor to *Writer's Digest* magazine, and his articles on writing have been widely anthologized. His diverse magazine publishing credits include *The Yacht, NurseWeek, Law and Order, Editor and Publisher, U.S. Catholic* and *The American Legion Magazine*.

His short stories have appeared in literary magazines such as *Northeast, Quarry West, Ascent*, and *Pub* and in glossy publications such as *Working Mother*.

INDEX